Praise for

Captured By Vision: 101 Insights to Empower Your Congregation

With insights gleaned from four decades of work, George Bullard reaches down the throat of your pet idea for "capturing a vision" and turns it inside out. People don't "capture a vision" he explains with wit, wisdom and anecdote, they are "captured by vision." Bullard's latest book convincingly explains how to put yourself in the position of willing and receptive captive.

--Norman Jameson, www.WordsandDeeds.me

An insightful book that keeps you focused and gives you hope. Vision is a team effort (not egocentric); arises from spiritual discernment (not brainstorming); results in spiritual vitality and mission (not bland statements and institutional survival). These insights and much more awaits your discovery in this practical book to help churches live into God's future.

Among his uniquely useful insights, George reaches into his long experience to coach how churches renew vision over the years. And he identifies not only what helps you move forward, but what holds you back. This is an essential resource for congregational and regional leaders.

--Thomas G. "Tom" Bandy, www.ThrivingChurch.com

George Bullard has done what only George can do—make a complex concept like vision approachable and understandable to all of us who care and love the Church. Pithy, practical and powerful are the words that kept coming to mind as I read through this book. I marked nearly every page with a note to return later to think more deeply about what was said. Any church seeking to discern their future needs to read this book.

--William G. "Bill" Wilson, The Center for Healthy Churches, www.CHChurches.org

George Bullard is the premier church consultant of his generation. Forty years of work with every imaginable kind of congregation and church organization has uniquely qualified him and blessed him with hard-won wisdom. You hold in your hands a marvelous distillation of that wisdom! Read this book carefully, reflect on it, allow it to get inside you and your congregation, and it will transform you. I commend this book to every Christian leader, clergy and lay, who wants to see congregations grow and thrive in faithfulness and effectiveness.

--Richard L. "Dick" Hamm, Former General Minister and President of the Christian Church (Disciples of Christ) in the US & Canada, www.Disciples.org

George Bullard is among the most experienced and talented interpreters of congregational life in our time. *Captured by Vision* is the culmination of his understanding of the importance of vision for church life and is filled with thoughtful, practical, realistic, and Spirit-filled suggestions for embracing God's vision for your congregation. His 101 statements of vision will transform a leadership core committed to a new future. His suggestions of how to accomplish them are "on target." I recommend it enthusiastically.

--Larry L. McSwain, Professor of Leadership (retired), McAfee School of Theology, Mercer University in Atlanta, www.Theology.Mercer.edu

"We know a thing or two because we've seen a thing or two," says the Farmers Insurance commercial. *Captured by Vision* is a wise companion for church leaders because George Bullard has seen 101 things about congregational vision firsthand.

George's vast experience takes readers on a grand pilgrimage into how vision is found and followed. Some of George's insights are surprises, some are counter-intuitive, but all feed leaders' spirits. There are too many guidelines to master quickly, so let *Captured by Vision* soak in slowly and deeply. It will open your eyes and heart to God's future for your church.

--Robert "Bob" Dale, Prolific Writer and Wise Teacher

A difficult part of the visioneering process is how to go about clarifying, casting, and implementing the vision itself. There must be a "vision for visioneering;" a way to imagine how church vision flows from leadership to congregation. *Captured By Vision* provides what is often a missing element to the visioning process.

George provides a wealth of insight in a concise and systematic approach that will simultaneously inspire creativity for big picture thinkers as they dream of "what could be," instruct analytical thinkers with reasons "why it should be," and provide process thinkers with steps for "how it can be."

--Kevin D. Glenn, Author of *Hand Over Fist: An Invitation to Civility*, Pastor of Calvary Baptist Church of Las Cruces, New Mexico, www.KevinGlenn.net

George has given the church of today and tomorrow a real gift as he shares his wisdom gained through his decades of consulting with churches. The bite-sized approach to sharing heavy truths is masterfully crafted to provide pastors and lay leaders points for prayer, reflection and action. *Captured By Vision* is truly a treasure of truths that inspire, encourage and guide!

--Edward "Eddie" Hammett, www.TransformingSolutions.org

Captured By Vision is a wonderful book to enable congregations to experience vision from God rather than finding vision in their programs structure. The church with true vision is contagious and more interested in people than programs. George effectively explains empowering vision from God as a grace gift where congregational vision results in disciplemaking.

--James "Jim" Royston, Retired Pastor and Denominational Executive

Having served with George Bullard off and on for 20 years, I have witnessed a man devoted to clarifying the challenge with the language of vision, its source, its impact and its necessity. George captures what I have watched him refine for at least two decades. This book clarifies the beauty, the process and means for receiving a revelation of God's vision.

Suitable for any church, this nondenominational tool ratchets away at the too often difficult task of visioning. Theologically sound, and life tested in multiple areas by a man used mightily of God.

--John Bost, Master Counsel Business Solutions

George Bullard addresses one of the most critical and misunderstood aspects of congregational and organizational life—vision. He destroys the myths around visionary leadership by taking the vision *off the page* and allow it to live and breathe. Vision is caught not taught. Bullard understands this and shows us the way forward. He doesn't just talk about vision; he takes you there allowing it to emerge from the passion of God's people as they join God's mission.

A must read for congregational leaders who desire to see their congregations live into the complex times we are in.

--Gary V Nelson, President, Tyndale University College & Seminary, www. Tyndale.ca

George Bullard understands that vision must be caught not coerced. In this book, he demonstrates how pastors and church leaders can receive a vision from God and empower their congregations to move forward in today's present realities. With profound insight drawn from years of real-life experience as a consultant, coach, and colleague, Bullard fills an important void missing in most congregational leadership books and offers wisdom for the renewal of the church.

--William D. "Bill" Shiell, President, Northern Seminary, www.Seminary.edu

As an experienced congregational consultant, George Bullard understands well the theoretical dimensions of vision. He also writes as someone familiar with the complexity of congregations to realize all vision models require rigorous review and adaptation considering those complexities. His ideas will ring true for clergy and lay leaders seeking to discern God's will for their congregations—freeing churches to what is fitting and faithful in their context.

--Lovett H. Weems, Jr., Lewis Center for Church Leadership, Wesley Theological Seminary, www.ChurchLeadership.org

Once again George Bullard gets to the heart of the matter. Congregations who understand that the ministry and mission of the church is a spiritual enterprise and an ongoing dance with the Living God are effective in doing the transforming work of the Gospel. *Captured by Vision* is solid guidance in an easy to use package. Get it and get better at understanding what you are called to do and how to do it well.

--Bruce A. Barkhauer, Minister for Faith and Giving, Christian Church (Disciples of Christ), www.CenterforFaithandGiving.org

George has captured enriching insights into finding and living into God's vision for a congregation. Through his years of experience and his own intense listening to the voice of God in his journey, he provides practical ideas for pastors and church leaders to listen for the vision that God has given for their unique situation. Too often, we wait for one charismatic person to deliver God's vision for us or see what another church is doing to fuel our vision. *Captured By Vision* challenges our perceived ideas about vision, and helps us recapture the New Testament pattern for vision development.

--Ken Kessler, Leader, Baptist General Association of Virginia Coaching Network, www.BGAV.org

CAPTURED *by* VISION

101 Insights to Empower
Your Congregation

George W. Bullard Jr.

Strategic Leadership Coach

www.BullardJournal.org

WESTBOW
PRESS®
A DIVISION OF THOMAS NELSON
& ZONDERVAN

Author Credits: Strategic Leadership Coach

Scripture taken from the NEW AMERICAN STANDARD BIBLE®, Copyright © 1960,1962,1963,1968,1971,1972,1973,1975,1977,19 95 by The Lockman Foundation. Used by permission.

Scripture taken from the King James Version of the Bible.

WestBow Press books may be ordered through booksellers or by contacting:

WestBow Press
A Division of Thomas Nelson & Zondervan
1663 Liberty Drive
Bloomington, IN 47403
www.westbowpress.com
1 (866) 928-1240

ISBN: 978-1-5127-6986-9 (sc)
ISBN: 978-1-5127-6988-3 (hc)
ISBN: 978-1-5127-6987-6 (e)

Library of Congress Control Number: 2016921357

Print information available on the last page.

WestBow Press rev. date: 01/09/2017

I dedicate this book to my ministry partners
with The Columbia Partnership, Inc. which was
active in collaborative ministry
2005-2017

Dick Hamm
Eddie Hammett
Norman Jameson
Ken Kessler
Jim Royston

It was a great ride and we did many things to contribute to the
vitality and vibrancy of congregations and denominations.

Our vision was,
To transform the capacity of the North American Church
to pursue and sustain vital Christ-centered ministry

Contents

Preface

The father of post-World War II effective church consulting, Lyle E. Schaller, was my most helpful consulting mentor. He spoke prophetically into my life. He taught me amazing things about congregations—how to consult with them, and how to bring about change within them. He was way ahead of the wave of strategic leadership coaching in his ability to ask penetrating and powerful questions that led congregations to think about possibilities they had not openly considered.

He lived a full and meaningful life as the foremost church consultant in North America for more than four decades, and served as an ongoing mentor to many people for even longer. He died in the spring of 2015 just a month short of his 92nd birthday.

In the early years of forming my approach to consulting with congregations, I based many things on his writings. As I approached strategic planning with congregations, I was especially impressed by his book, *The Local Church Looks to the Future,* first published in 1968. That is until I met Lyle in 1978 and began receiving training and mentoring directly from him.

Sitting with Lyle at lunch one day at the Yokefellow Institute in Richmond, IN, I praised him for the training I was receiving. Then I told him I thought what I was learning was contradictory to his book, *The Local Church Looks to the Future*. Lyle told me I was right. He did not believe what he said in that book any more.

"But Lyle," I said. "I saw this book for sale in a bookstore within the past two weeks."

"Oh, I believe in eating," proclaimed Lyle. "I have not asked my publisher to withdraw any books from store shelves. I have just moved on and do not believe what I said in that book. It does not work."

He went on to explain that too many congregations read his book, appointed a committee, and gave them the task of coming up with a written mission, purpose, core values, and vision. They brought forward long documents, and then were weary and stopped their planning efforts without ever taking positive, forward action.

His intention was that congregations would be inspired to engage in transformational ministry action that would increase their vitality and vibrancy. This did not happen, so he knew his concept of the ideal did not work in real life.

At that point he changed his approach to focus on action-oriented ministry, and then reflection on what vision God might be seeking to impart to and through congregations. This dramatically increased his effectiveness and helped congregations soar to new heights.

His perspective also changed my approach over the years. It did not decrease the foundational importance of vision. It primarily changed the timing for seeking to help congregations become captured by vision. That which is most important does not always come first. There is a priority of urgency and there is a priority around timing.

I continue to appreciate the foundational importance of being captured by God's empowering vision. I now understand it is not the first thing that needs to happen in the clear majority of congregational situations I encounter.

- **Words and Ideas:** What is "God's empowering vision" for a congregation?

My exchange 40 years ago with Lyle Schaller has many implications for congregations. Here are a four.

First, it is not as important to have a well-crafted, written statement of vision as it is that you are captured by God's empowering vision for your congregation. Empowering actions that create forward ministry progress are more important than an exceptional statement of vision. Words will come when it is time.

Second, while being captured by God's empowering vision for your congregation is the most important aspect of the forward movement of your congregation, it may not be the first thing congregations need to focus on when seeking to make forward ministry progress. It may be the second, third, or fourth. It depends.

Third, if you do not engage in actions that result in forward ministry progress, even the most articulate statement of vision is worthless. It is not what you say you feel led to do, it is what you do that makes the difference. Talk is still cheap. Actions still speak louder than words.

Fourth, people who are gifted at crafting an inspiring vision statement may not be good at taking action. People who are gifted at taking action to fulfill God's empowering vision might not be able to write a coherent vision statement. Congregations need both types of spiritual gifts and skills, and need to celebrate both types of people.

--George Bullard
Columbia, SC
January 2017

Acknowledgements

I am thankful for a faithful, effective, and innovative network of teachers, mentors, coaches, and learners who have impacted my ministry, and permitted me to arrive at a place where I believe I have something significant to say about God's empowering vision for congregations.

As you have already seen in the Preface, I am grateful for the life and ministry of Lyle E. Schaller who impacted my life through his writing, speaking, and personal ministry to me for 50 years. Beyond Lyle, there were numerous mentors in my early years of ministry who contributed to my formation. During my seminary days and beyond I was impacted by Willis Bennett, Larry McSwain, and Russell Bennett. Like Lyle, Larry McSwain is a person who impacted me for many decades.

Colleagues and supervisors at the national missions agency of my denomination who also continued to be part of my life were Don Hammer and Jere Allen. Ministry colleagues whose questions and supervision positively impacted me were Burtt Potter, Lawrence Childs, Glenn Akins, Bob Dale, Ray Rust, Carlisle Driggers, and Jim Royston. Through The Columbia Partnership, which is where I have primarily hung my hat for the past 12 years, I am grateful for Dick Hamm, Eddie Hammett, Norman Jameson, Ken Kessler, and Jim Royston.

Numerous people mentored me from afar through their writings and speaking. With each these I had one or more chances to meet with them and enjoy conversation. They include Kennon Callahan, Ezra Earl Jones, Speed Leas, Loren Mead, Jim Collins, and Peter Drucker. Others could also be mentioned.

While I realize many of these names are unfamiliar to you, it is important to me to mention them, and to express my appreciation for their God-given gifts that have spoken into my life.

Regarding this manuscript, I am especially thankful to Norman Jameson who is a friend, colleague, journalist, and gifted writer. Any writing he touches is amazingly better. I appreciate him serving as the editor of this book. The only thing that would have been better is for him to have written this book from the first word forward, rather than having to improve my writing style to make it come alive and be more readable for you.

Nine friends read the manuscript to provide their impressions. I am grateful for the gift of their insights and reflections. Six of the nine persons were church laypersons. That was intentional so we could take this book and turn it into something more readable and impressionable for laypersons who might read it and study it in small groups in congregations.

These readers were Ann Fleshman, Gilda Bocock, Jeffrey Collins, J. C. Ballew, Kim Sanders, Kay Bissette, Dan Wilkinson, David Jones, and Ken Kessler.

Throughout this book illustrations of congregations and leaders are shared—especially at the beginning of chapters. While these are real congregations and leaders, typically any names used are not the real names of these congregations and leaders. In a few places, they are identified, or a source is referenced that tells their story. Congregations and leaders change so quickly, that I have referenced how they expressed themselves when I experienced them. In some cases, I had many years of observation of them, and in other cases it was just one day or a weekend.

I have saved my family for last. Reference to them should never be trite or insignificant. Their importance is beyond measure. I am extremely grateful for the grounding my parents gave me. G. W. and Mozelle Bullard were involved in congregational and denominational ministry for their entire lives. I learned so much directly from them, and by spiritual and intellectual osmosis.

My wife, Betty, and my children Jonathan and Allison sacrificed time with their husband and father for me to gain the experience and insight that allowed me to write this book. At the same time, we were always committed to one another, loved one another, and had great times together. My children would even travel with me to congregational retreats I was leading and got to where they could give some of my speeches as well as I could.

Introduction

Congregational Vision is About Seeing Jesus with Your Heart, Soul, Mind, and Strength

My mother, Mozelle Bridgers Bullard, was a person of great Christian vision and insight. She could see Jesus with her heart, soul, mind, and strength even when she could not see Him with her eyes.

Among the many ministries in her life was a prayer and greeting card ministry that by my estimation focused on over 300 people. This involved a wall calendar she hung in her kitchen. On that calendar were the names of individuals and couples on the day of their birthday and wedding anniversary.

A week or so before their special day my mother would purchase a card for each person, write a caring note on it, and place it in the mail to them. On their special day, usually at 10:00 a.m., my mother would be on her knees beside her bed praying for these people. For those who knew not only about the card they received, but the prayer that was offered, it was an important and inspiring life comfort and encouragement from Mozelle Bullard.

During the last decade of my mother's life, she suffered from macular degeneration. It was slow moving, but the procedures available at the time could not stop—much less reverse—its impact on her eyesight. Gradually she lost the sharpness of her eyesight, then some of her forward vision, and eventually she lost all central vision.

In the last few years of her life she could no longer see to write her cards and letters. She had to depend on family members and a woman who spent a half-day with her several days each week.

Simultaneously, my mother had multiple types of arthritis that were progressing in her body, and particularly impacting the functioning of her hands, feet, and knees. The result was she also got to the point where she could not kneel by her bed to offer heartfelt prayers from a true follower of Jesus.

While this did not stop her from praying sitting in her favorite chair, it was not the same. Her inability to shop for cards, write notes, see that they were mailed, and kneel by her bed to pray for these people, caused her to feel her life had lost a sense of purpose.

She started thinking about her life situation very deeply. She did not verbalize this to me when I talked with her. One day when her pastor was visiting she did verbalize her feelings of despair to him.

Mike was a very caring and wise pastor. He was a great person with whom she could talk. She asked him, "Mike, is it alright if I pray that I die?"

He thought for a moment or two. Then he said to her, "No, Mozelle, it is not alright if you pray that you die. But it is alright if you pray that the will of God might be done about your life and death."

My mother had not lost insightful vision. She had just lost significant eyesight. My mother, although she could clearly see Jesus with her full heart, soul, mind, and strength, could not have the vital and vibrant life she longed for without also literally walking by sight.

She could not look clearly at the face of people she loved. The clarity of her memory of those faces was fading. While she could see Jesus with her heart, she could no longer clearly see Jesus in the faces of people she loved and was called anew to love.

My mother's situation has implications for your congregation. Here are three.

First, true vision involves the ability to see Jesus in people and situations with your full heart, soul, mind, and strength. This is deeper than seeing them with just your eyes. To see Jesus in people is seeing the depth of who they are as people of potential and followers of Jesus.

Second, if we only look on the outward appearance we may not see the ability of the unconditional love of Jesus to transform people and situations. We must see the Jesus potential in the lives of people we encounter.

Third, as loving people we need to see evidence of what the unconditional love of Jesus does not only in the heart, soul, mind, and strength of people who accept His love, but also how it changes the expression on their faces.

Congregations Without Vision Cannot See Jesus

Seeing Jesus is a powerful image in the New Testament. Matthew 25:37-40 says,

> "Then the righteous will answer Him, 'Lord, when did we see You hungry, and feed You, or thirsty, and give You something to drink? And when did we see You a stranger, and invite You in, or naked, and clothe You? When did we see You sick, or in prison, and come to You?' The King will answer and say to them, 'Truly I say to you, to the extent that you did it to one of these brothers of Mine, even the least of them, you did it to Me.'" (NASB)

It takes not only vision with our eyes, but vision with our full senses. It is not just literally seeing an object, but seeing an opportunity. It is not just about your eyesight, but is also about your experience. Your congregation needs vision or it may not be able to see and fully experience Jesus.

Every congregation needs God's empowering vision. It is not optional. Why? Because vision will empower the forward progress of your congregation and allow you to see the Jesus potential in people. Without vision many congregations tread water seeking to avoid drowning. Many congregations are blind to the hungry, thirsty, stranger, naked, sick, and imprisoned.

While your congregation needs God's empowering vision, up to 80 percent of all congregations are missing it. They make successful programs and a met budget their vision, not realizing these are not the substance of a vision from God. Growing numerically is not necessarily the same as fulfilling God's empowering vision.

Some congregations believe vision equals being healthy—which is partially true. Some congregations believe vision is successfully attracting a target audience, such as young adult families—which also is partially true.

Some congregations believe vision is about growing numerically—which at times is a side benefit of a clear empowering vision. Some congregations believe vision is about becoming missional—which is a great characteristic of many congregations with vision.

At the risk of being accused of spiritualizing this issue—as if that was a bad thing—every congregation needs God's empowering vision. Every pastor, staff minister, and layperson needs a life and ministry full of visionary energy. Anything less than living in the light of God's empowering vision is inadequate.

Notice I did not say your pastor needs vision, although he or she does. Pastors need vision for their life and ministry. Pastors need the empowerment of vision in their lives. A pastor's vision for his or her congregation and the vision congregations need for themselves is not always the same thing. God's empowering vision for your congregation is always the best vision.

Some years ago I spoke to a couple of hundred ministry leaders in a regional denominational organization. The executive director of that organization came to me at the end and said, "How do congregations develop vision?"

Many congregations, and those who consult with or coach them, cannot figure out vision. They know they need one, but they do not know how to get there. They want Dr. Feelgood to pull into town with his medicine show and sell them an elixir that will produce vision. There is not one, so don't swallow what he's selling.

Perhaps vision is part of God's grace gift to us. This would mean vision is not something we earn, or an exercise we complete. It is a grace gift of God we discern, and when we make ourselves open and vulnerable, it can capture us.

- **Words and Ideas:** What does it mean to "discern" or to have "discernment?"

Too many times congregations see vision as something organizational. That is unfortunate, because congregations are living, breathing, moving, dynamic, ever-changing spiritual organisms and not organizations. They see the pithy mottos and slogans of some businesses and say, "I want one of those." Or, they see the well-developed professional visions of large congregations or Christian ministries and think they will fit their congregation.

Questions for Your Congregation

First, is it possible your congregation understands the need for vision, but is trying too hard on its own to acquire vision? Perhaps better than directly seeking vision is the journey to see Jesus in the interactions of the congregation with one another, and in the faces of the people to whom God is sending you.

Second, has your congregation brought secular organizational success perspectives into the church by considering vision to be the success of programs and budget? Certainly these can be positive vital signs, but are they truly a vision from God for a spiritual organism?

Third, does your congregation want to avoid its responsibility and opportunity to be captured by God's empowering vision by saying it is the pastor's responsibility to provide vision? Do you want your pastor to ascend a holy mountain and come down with a vision?

101 Insights to Empower Your Congregation

This book contains 101 congregational vision insights. They have been developed over many years of focusing on congregational vision and my work with hundreds of congregations and denominational entities of many stripes. I have organized the 101 congregational vision insights around nine chapters as follows:

1. What is Vision? *Vision is a Movement of God that is Memorable*
2. God's Role in Vision. *May You Be with the Source*
3. Pastors and the Enduring Visionary Leadership Community. *Vision Casting is Everyone's Responsibility*
4. Vision—Written or Experienced? *Which Comes First: A Statement or an Experience?*
5. Excellent Versus Mediocre Visions. *Vision is Not About "Good Enough is Good Enough"*
6. Vision is not about Programs and Management. *Congregations Cannot Push Their Way Into God's Future*
7. Living into God's Empowering Vision. *Celebrate Vision Fulfillment Without Ceasing*
8. Vision Renewal. *Vision is Always Out of Sight*
9. Vision Killers. *Those Who Worship the Past Will Seek to Kill Vision*

A tenth chapter looks at various ways congregations can acquire vision. It is entitled Getting from Here to Vision. *"If one does not know to which port one is sailing, no wind is favorable." –Seneca, Roman Philosopher*

This is followed by a call to action for the reader called *Afterword*. Then a section of *Words and Ideas* will explain various words and ideas used in the text of this book rather than stopping the narrative flow to explain them. At the end is a full list of the 101 insights to empower your congregation.

About Reading This Book

Who?

A global understanding of who ought to read this book goes something like this: Anyone who is positively passionate about congregations being mobilized by God's empowering vision for their future ministry ought to read this book. If it is important to you that congregations not settle for what is "good enough," but seek to move prophetically toward God's full Kingdom potential, you ought to read this book.

You should read this book if your congregation is clueless about God's empowering vision. You are not sure what it is, few if any people in the congregation understand what it is, and no one seems to be seeking to discern or cast God's empowering vision.

This book is for you if your congregation has a motto members can recite on cue, even in the middle of the night, but no clear sense of God's spiritual and strategic direction for the future of the congregation. Your congregation may have branded its identity, but that is not the same thing as being captured by God's empowering vision.

Does your congregation long to embark on a journey to discover God's empowering vision? Do you want to be more than you are? Do you want to move beyond "good enough" to "exceptional" in meeting the real needs, of real people, in real time?

Has it been seven or more years since your congregation engaged in an in-depth process to discover or rediscover the empowering vision God has for it? If your congregation is at least 21 years old, and has completed its first generation life, it must renew its vision every seven years or risk decline.

- **Words and Ideas:** Why is "21 years or the first generation of a congregation" so significant?

You ought to read this book if your congregation is less than a generation old, or just starting, to be sure you are well grounded in living into God's empowering vision. It is also very important to anticipate a future point where renewal of your founding vision, no matter how passionate you were about it, is a process whose time has come.

If we place these descriptions of "who" into people categories it would involve pastors, staff persons, lay leaders, denominational staff, consultants, coaches, college professors, seminary and divinity school professors, other third-party providers to congregations, and students preparing for ministry service with congregations. If any of these is you, then I hope you will read this book before putting yourself into a position to suggest how congregations ought to acquire and live into God's empowering vision.

When and How?

While it is obvious individuals ought to read this book in their own way, in their own place, and at their own pace, I want to go beyond this.

Pastors and church staff teams ought to read this book and talk about it as a team. They should consider how they ought to lead their congregation in their unique situation to become captured by God's empowering vision. Maybe this is not the way they've always thought. They may need to rethink their role as the creators and casters of vision, and see how they can be part of God's empowering of vision throughout their congregation.

Lay leadership teams should spend some time in dialogue and prayer about vision for their congregation while simultaneously reading this book. This could be a great way for pastors and church staff teams to initiate a vision discernment process in their congregation.

This book could also be taught to large numbers of lay leaders and general congregational participants through classes and small groups reading it. One suggestion is that a number of people equal to at least 21 percent of the average number of people present on a typical weekend for worship ought to read and dialogue about this book in preparation for a journey of discovery regarding God empowering vision.

CHAPTER ONE

What is Vision?

Vision is a movement of God that is memorable

At a national conference, I was leading a breakout session on helping congregations reach their full Kingdom potential. I went around the room asking people to introduce themselves and tell why they chose this session from the list of others available. When I came to one pastor, I had an idea what he would say because I had heard him say it before. I smiled knowing what was coming. He introduced himself and said, "I am here because George Bullard ruined my life."

I led his staff in a two-day retreat some years earlier at a time they were in a transition period in their congregational life. They were trying to discover what was next. The concepts with which I challenged them caused them to rethink how they led their congregation. They needed to become captured by a new empowering vision from God. I pointed them in a possible direction and they went forward with great zeal.

What the pastor meant when he said I ruined his life is that he was comfortable prior to the retreat, but after the retreat he had to roll up his sleeves and get to work about a new sense of direction. During the retreat his staff lovingly confronted him as both their friend and their supervisor, and suggested that for them to move forward he needed to change and write a new chapter in his ministry.

He responded positively to this challenge. His was an "old first church" in the center of the city. The impact on his ministry and the life of his congregation was tremendously productive, meaningful, and significant. They became a positive model for other congregations.

One factor that eased their ability to move forward was that the staff got it about vision. They already knew the answer to the question posed in this chapter," What is Vision?" Knowing that answer is a foundational issue for congregations who desire to become captured by God's empowering vision.

Many people, other than me, played a role in the significant future of this congregation. I recommend you read about the rest of the story. Pick up the book *Hopeful Imagination: Traditional Churches Finding God's Way in a Changing World* (Nurturing Faith, 2014).

Congregational Vision is a Grace Gift of God We Discern

When I first started consulting on vision more than 40 years ago, I had a very left-brained approach. This was natural for me, because I am a hopelessly left-brained person. This meant I focused more on the vision statement than on the characteristics or qualities of vision. It meant I was more focused on being sure vision was crafted first before other things in a strategic planning process.

I have transitioned in my own perspective over the past several decades. I am now much more right-brained in my approach to vision. I talk more about the feelings and experiences of vision, rather than the statement, strategy, or structure of vision. I talk more about vision emerging out of a "ready, shoot, then aim" process that is chaordic and allows vision to reflect the actions in which God engages us.

- **Words and Ideas:** What is the meaning of the word "chaordic," and why is it important in the search for God's empowering vision?

Vision is now for me much more about telling a congregation's future story of ministry rather than crafting a 15 or fewer word statement that emerges out of a smoke-filled back room where a committee meets.

During the last decades of the 20th century many organizations focused on following the example of a visionary leader. The individual who held the position of highest office in the organization was the person who needed to provide, cast, and embody the vision.

You may remember the multiple commercials in which automobile executive Lee Iacocca was the embodiment as well as the spokesperson of the vision for the Chrysler Corporation. It was a strong example during those decades. More recent examples would be Steve Jobs with Apple, Bill Gates with Microsoft, and Mark Zuckerberg with Facebook.

A carryover was that congregations emphasized the ideal of a senior or solo pastor who could bring vision to the congregation, and direct the congregation forward in a manner like Lee Iacocca for Chrysler.

How many times have you heard someone in your congregation say when they are between pastors, "We need a pastor who will bring us vision and get us moving forward?"

Vision is not the pastor pushing the congregation forward. It is allowing the congregation to be pulled forward by God. Of course, a new pastor with a new vision—or an old vision he or she brought from their last church—wants to push a congregation forward and make it "successful" beyond what it has recently experienced. But what happens if that vision is not God's empowering vision, but merely the goal of a pastor who brings a formula to his or her new congregation?

While the following statement may be over-simplistic, it is appropriate to suggest that part of being captured by vision is "letting go and letting God." The implication is that often we feel like we must push a congregation forward with our own abilities rather than being embraced by the grace gift of God through the presence of the Holy Spirit pulling us forward.

We mistakenly feel we must work more, push harder, and force something great to happen. Sometimes we feel like we've got to take the reins of control away from God's Holy Spirit because God is moving too slowly and we know better how to move our congregation forward. We see our efforts and timing as better than those of the Triune God.

You fool! This day the life of your congregation will be required of you.

Prayer discernment is needed. While it is possible to overemphasize waiting on the Lord and seeking discernment, and while I suggest a much more proactive approach when I work with congregations and denominations on vision, in many situations we need more prayerful discernment.

Vision is not an organizational statement. Usually what congregational vision committees produce is not vision, but a program and management statement that fits an organization rather than a congregation. The focus should be on congregations as spiritual organisms.

Vision is part of God's grace gift to us, and not a series of steps or deeds that produce vision. Vision is not something we earn, or an exercise we complete.

The exercises around vision do have a purpose. They help us discern strategies and tactics for living into our vision. They themselves are not the vision, nor do the exercises reveal true vision. Ultimately vision captures our spiritual imagination.

This has three implications for your congregation:

First, vision is more likely to emerge from a process of writing the future story of ministry for your congregation than from the expert crafting of a vision statement.

Second, vision does not appear because we push harder, but because we listen to God with a spirit of discernment.

Third, because vision is a grace gift of God. We cannot earn it. We can receive it and rejoice in it.

Vision is a Movement of God That is Memorable

How do you define vision? If you cannot define it, you may not know what it is when you have it. Vision is not the same as mission. The eternal mission of a congregation is the timeless understanding of the past, present, and future focus for congregations in general as they seek to carry out the Great Commission in the spirit of the Great Commandment.

Vision is not the same as purpose. The everlasting purpose of a congregation is the past to present understanding of the reason a congregation came into existence. Why was it founded? What was its historic purpose? Why was it needed? What was that first empowering vision from God that fueled the forward progress of the congregation?

Core values are extremely important in congregations, but they are not vision. Enduring core values are the Christian principles based on the life and teachings of Jesus preserved for us in the Bible that are uniquely expressed within a congregation. What is at the center of your congregation that like a divining rod guides you to the core, essential understandings of what it means in your situation to be a Christ-centered, faith-based community living into God's empowering vision?

Vision is the current understanding of the spiritual and strategic journey of God for a congregation over the next seven years or longer. Vision empowers the future. It is about the pulling of God rather than the pushing of humankind. It fuels the forward progress of congregations. It takes congregations beyond the current horizon to places they cannot yet see, and may not ever reach.

- **Words and Ideas:** Check out additional characteristics of planning language that involve "mission," "purpose," "core values," and "vision."

Here are seven *Vision Insights* that address the question, "What is vision?"

Vision Insight 001: Vision is a movement of God that is memorable rather than a statement of humankind that is memorized.

George W. Bullard Jr.

Vision is about God's Holy Spirit moving among us and touching us with inspiration, opening a door for us to walk through, or showing us something that helps us say, "I see it!" It is sensing and feeling the movement of God's Holy Spirit that allows us to see and focus on God's future for us with our full heart, soul, mind, and strength.

Vision is not a statement, although it may at some point be expressed in a statement for sharing with others. True vision is seldom experienced first in the form of a statement. Vision is not something we memorize and recite on cue. We do not read it from a book or a worship folder. Vision is more about feeling the earth move under our feet at a James Taylor and Carole King performance than reading the lyrics to the song *I Feel the Earth Move*.

Vision Insight 002: Vision is the *current* understanding of God's spiritual and strategic journey for a congregation.

It is not yesterday's understanding of God's spiritual and strategic journey. It is our current understanding. As we move along our spiritual and strategic journey our understanding of vision will mature, transition, and change.

Vision emerges from discerning the movement of God within a congregation. It answers the question, "What is God saying to our congregation about our future?" It is the *current* understanding, knowing that the understanding of congregations can change, move deeper, become more prophetic, and be felt clearer as congregations continually listen to the voice of God.

Vision Insight 003: Vision is about walking by faith in God rather than by what is in plain sight, as we are admonished in 2 Corinthians 5:7.

This Corinthians verse admonishes us to walk by faith rather than by sight. Another way to say this is that we need to walk by faith in God's sight, or what God can see that we cannot yet see, or what God understands that we do not yet understand.

Walking by faith is seeing God's empowering vision with our full heart, soul, mind and strength. It is about the ability to see Jesus in the eyes of the hungry, thirsty, stranger, naked, sick and imprisoned. Without the sight that faith gives us, we are unlikely to be captured by God's empowering vision.

We must resist the temptation for our vision to be the one we see in any other congregation. God's empowering vision for us is unique. Will Mancini in his book *Church Unique: How Missional Leaders Cast Vision, Capture Culture, and Create Movement* (Jossey-Bass, 2008) explains that "each church has a culture that reflects its particular values, thoughts, attitudes, and actions and shows how church leaders can unlock their church's individual DNA and unleash their congregation's one-of-a-kind potential." (From the inside flap of the book cover.)

Vision Insight 004: Vision is not what leaders cast and followers catch. It is something by which leaders and followers are captured.

Vision is not something where leaders say, "We've got to get us one of those." Then hold a meeting, workshop, or retreat, and conclude with a vision written on newsprint and taped to the wall. Acquiring vision is not an event. It is an experience. Events may set goals, strategies, and tactics. Experiences reveal vision.

Vision is something revealed in a breakthrough experience or when we search for God's direction for our congregation. We do not catch vision. We are captured by it.

You do not acquire vision passively. It is a full-contact, all hands on deck, congregational body experience. Anyone and everyone in a congregation can be captured by God's empowering vision. In the clear majority of cases those who are seriously seeking God's vision will be the first to be captured by it.

Vision Insight 005: Vision is about seeing with your full heart, soul, mind, and strength, rather than with only your eyes—even with corrective lenses.

Vision is a body and soul experience, not a mind game. If we can see our future with our eyes it is not God's empowering vision. Vision is seen with spiritual imagination.

Too many congregations believe making their practice of ministry more faithful and efficient is sufficient to declare they have vision. They believe if they can see the implications of what they are already doing better than they do now, then they will discover they already have vision.

That is an exercise in catching hold of our vision rather than being captured by God's empowering vision.

Vision Insight 006: Moses did not see vision in the burning bush. He experienced it with his whole being and was transformed by it.

Moses had a full body and soul experience as he encountered God in the form of the burning bush. Few have ever had such a dramatic experience through which they were captured by God's empowering vision.

In the spirit of Jewish theologian Martin Buber, the encounter Moses had with God on Mt. Sinai was an *I-Thou* experience. But when he sought to recount the experience to the Israelites it transitioned into an *I-It* experience because it was not their experience. (See Martin Buber, *I and Thou,* Martino Publishing 2010. First published in German in 1923 and first published in English in 1937.)

I-Thou is when we have a genuine encounter with God. *I-It* is when we do storytelling that recounts our *I-Thou* experience. Master storytellers can thrill us with how artfully they share their craft, but it is still a story about something, and not the actual real-time experience.

Vision Insight 007: Vision is the super high-octane fuel that drives the spiritual and strategic journey of a congregation.

Vision is not about regular congregational life. It is about high octane life. High octane life under the leadership of the Triune God is often a faster paced and a more significantly changed life that can lead to congregational transformation.

It is not business as usual. It is about high performance congregational life. High performance congregational life focuses as much on the quality of what is done as it does the quantity. It focuses on significance as much as it does success.

It is not about seeking common ground. It takes a congregation to higher ground. Congregations who focus on higher ground are concerned not only with making sure the life and ministry of their congregation connects with the common themes that draw their congregation into deeper and more positive community. They also challenge their congregation to soar to places they have never been before. This is higher ground. Common ground is inadequate.

Key Points for Your Congregation

First, even the best crafted vision statement does not a vision make. Vision is a memorable movement and not a memorized statement. Focus not on words, but experiences where God's empowering vision is felt.

Second, look for vision with your full heart, soul, mind, and strength rather than only your eyes. Your eyes can play tricks on you.

Third, vision transforms. It is about more than just transition and change. Be ready for a wild, prophetic ride if you truly want vision rather than just programmatic success.

Call to Action for Your Congregation

Begin praying for a movement in your congregation that represents God's empowering vision, is a movement that is memorable, and is something to which you can give your full heart, soul, mind, and strength. If you are not the pastor, volunteer to work with your pastor to put together a discernment process with the pastor's initiating leadership.

George W. Bullard Jr.

A Prayer for Your Congregation

Oh, God, our help in ages past, our hope for years to come, help us to see Your empowering vision as a grace gift. We cannot earn it. We cannot buy it. We can only discern and receive it. May we see it as important enough to discern it as Your miraculous movement within our congregation, and not a simplistic catchy statement we write. May Your empowering vision not occur as a moment within our congregation, but as a movement that is memorable. In Your Holy name we pray. Amen.

CHAPTER TWO

God's Role in Vision

May you be with the source

Western Boulevard was a congregation in a transitional neighborhood near downtown. Survival was a major concern. They reached a point when they knew if they could not find something that worked to bring them greater vitality and vibrancy, they might not be alive in a few years.

Vision was not a subject they responded to easily in this working-class and welfare-dependent transitional neighborhood. Something short-term that would simply help them survive until next year was more acceptable. With that in mind, the fear of not surviving was the motivational tool the pastor and staff used to get the congregation to address the challenges of their neighborhood with positive missional engagement.

It worked. They were pleased to help their neighborhood, liked the new activity around the church, and especially liked the new people who started attending. It gave them hope. Yet, it still did not give them vision.

One day an unlikely member confronted the pastor and accused him of lying to the congregation. He accused the pastor of telling the congregation they needed to reach out in their neighborhood so they could survive. The truth, this layman declared, was they did these things because that is what the love of Jesus would have them do.

11

The pastor smiled broadly. This was the first layperson in the congregation who gave verbal evidence of being captured by God's empowering vision. A couple of years earlier the pastor had stopped talking about vision because no one seemed to get it. Now the pastor was extremely pleased a layperson had connected with the source—God—and got it about vision.

This time when the pastor started preaching, teaching, and leading around God's empowering vision, the congregation got it. For the next seven years, they lived out a new sense of God's spiritual and strategic direction for the congregation.

The long-term story, however, is not as bright. After they lived into God's empowering vision for seven years, the vision waned, the congregation wandered in the wilderness of their neighborhood context, never dreamed a new dream again, and ultimately died about 15 years after the layperson confronted the pastor.

These dynamics—and why this happened—will become clear as we keep moving forward through the 101 insights.

When It Comes to Congregational Vision May You Be With the Source

"What we need is for God to audibly tell us where we need to be headed as a congregation," is a common refrain of laypersons and church staffers when they are frustrated about vision. "Then we will know. At least, God, give us a sign. Don't hold back on us!"

Other churches in transition say, "We need to get a new pastor who will bring us God's vision and get us moving in the right direction."

Or, if they're talking about their current pastor, lay leaders may say, "If we had a real pastor who had a vision for this congregation and would lead us to accomplish it, we could really be a great church."

And what I hear from pastors is, "These people will just not follow my vision. I need to move to another church where people are open and responsive to my vision."

Others say, "They did not teach me in seminary how to discern God's vision, just how to interpret God's visions expressed in the Bible. Not even my ordination process helped me understand I would be expected to bring God's vision to my congregation. Someone should have told me about my role regarding vision."

Still others, "I prayed and God gave me a vision for this church. I have tried and tried to cast this vision, but my congregation gives no evidence of hearing it."

Or, "We hired this great Christian consulting group who promised they would help us develop a vision statement around which we could organize all we do. The process was great and truly inspiring. The early results gave evidence of a true transformation of our congregation. But, a couple of years in it waned, and once again we are directionless."

These statements miss the point of the three forces of congregational vision. They are confusing the *source* of vision, the *casting* of vision, and the *ownership* of vision. For congregations to be truly captured by vision they must understand the forces of source, casting, and ownership. They must be able to see or sense vision, for as noted in the Introduction, congregations without vision cannot see Jesus.

It is a synergy of all three forces that is essential. This synergy probably happens in the order presented here.

Force One—The Source of Vision: The first force of vision is its source. From where does congregational vision originate? The simple answer is God. God is the source of all true vision for congregations.

It is not the pastor. It does not come out of the latest staff or board retreat. It does not come from the deacons or elders. It is not a committee—not even the pastor search committee or the staff parish relations committee. It is not in a playbook from a highly successful church. It is not in the latest business book or conference speaker's notes.

Any statement of vision by humankind that does not reflect a truly spiritual movement inspired in a congregation by God's empowering vision is only a statement. Remember, vision is a movement of God that is memorable rather than a statement of humankind that is memorized.

Force Two—The Casting of Vision: Whose responsibility is it to cast vision? Leaders have the key role, of course. The most important leader who casts vision is the senior or solo pastor. But, that does not make the pastor the *source* of vision. Leaders are the voices who cast the empowering vision God has inspired in them.

God is seeking to impart vision to the full congregation. We hope the pastor is among the first to be captured by God's empowering vision because he or she must continually cast that vision among the congregation.

Likewise, we hope other key leaders and people with positive spiritual passion are captured by vision and proactively support and provide additional voices for casting it.

Never does that make vision the pastor's vision or sole responsibility. It is always God's empowering vision for the congregation. Leaders are simply the ones casting the vision. The congregation is God's hands and feet.

- **Words and Ideas:** What does it mean to "cast" vision, and what are some examples of "casting?"

Force Three—The Ownership of Vision: Whose responsibility is it to own vision? The congregation must own the vision at a sufficient depth and breadth that members are passionate about fulfilling the vision. The desired result is not the destination, but the commitment to live into God's empowering vision and to journey towards that destination.

Never will 100 percent of a congregation own the vision. Yet it is essential that it is owned by at least 21 percent of the congregation who exhibit positive spiritual passion about the future toward which God is leading the congregation.

- **Words and Ideas:** What is the meaning of "21 percent," and what are some variations on this percentage?

It is essential that every possible program, ministry, and other actions of the congregation align with the vision God has given them.

It is these three: source, casting, and ownership. The greatest of these is source. Rather than adopting the phrase from Star Wars "May the force be with you," it is better to say, "May you be with the source."

The Only Vision That Works for Congregations is God's Empowering Vision

"The Triune God is the only true source of vision that is clearly spiritual and has any chance of pulling a congregation forward in the direction of its full Kingdom potential. Humankind has great ideas. Humankind has points of inspiration. Only God has vision that fully recognizes the future potential of a congregation that builds on its past and present.

At the same time God does not seem to impose vision, but to inspire vision. God clearly and powerfully helps us imagine what it will be like when we are fully captured by vision. Therefore, God is the author of vision in congregations." – A pastor candidate

When a lead pastor candidate said this to a search committee their hearts sank. They thought this person was their best candidate. They were looking forward to the vision he could bring to their church. His current congregation had soared under his leadership. Amid their disappointment they were not sure where they would turn next.

This represents the perspective of many congregations. They think great pastors bring vision and make the congregation soar. This idea is repeated so often that congregations believe it is true.

What if it is not true? What if the pastor is not the source of vision? What if God is the only reliable and faithful source?

Here are some *Vision Insights* that speak to my perspective on God's role in vision.

Vision Insight 008: The only vision that will work is God's empowering vision. Neither the pastor's vision nor the lay leadership's vision is sufficient.

The vision of the pastor, staff, or lay leaders is the vision of humankind. Often it is an organizational vision of success and not a spiritual organism vision of faithfulness, effectiveness, and innovation.

Vision by pastors, staff members, and lay leaders is typically either a short-term tactical vision or a grandiose vision that is more a fantasy than a clear look into the future. The vision of humankind is insufficient. The only sufficient, transformational vision is God's empowering vision.

Vision Insight 009: Vision is initiated by God to the body the church, cast by leadership, and owned by membership.

Pastors, staff members, and lay leadership do not initiate vision. They may initiate conversation, prayer, reflections, discernment processes, and actions to pursue vision. Only God initiates true vision.

God's initiation of vision does not happen because of calendar planning by congregational leadership. It happens in God's timing. True vision is a kairos experience rather than a chronos event. I have often felt it primarily happens when a congregation is ready to receive it and act on it.

- **Words and Ideas:** What do these terms "kairos" and "chronos" mean?

Vision Insight 010: Vision is more about the pulling of God into the future than the pushing of humankind to do better each year.

We all want to succeed at whatever we do. We all want to do better next year than we did this year or last year. But, God may want more from us. We may focus on short-term fixes. God focuses on long-term solutions.

Don't picture God pushing us and burdening us with external stress. See God as gently and continually pulling us forward. When we resist God's pulling or seek to do it ourselves, we create stress. When we respond to God's pulling it is stress free.

Vision Insight 011: One crucial test of vision is that it moves the congregation forward in God's image and not the image of humankind.

Discernment of the true, grace-filled direction for a congregation is an ongoing process that continually asks if each new major action is taking the congregation in the direction of fulfilling its God-given vision.

It is not about moving the congregation in the direction of any individual leader, the pastor and staff, the board or council, a certain age group, longer-tenured members, key influencers in the life of the congregation, or the people of the greatest spiritual passion about the congregation's future.

True vision continually visualizes the congregation in the image of God. Like a master artist God creates an ever-clearer image for a congregation with high definition that displays the image as multi-dimensional, dramatic, and impactful.

God's Empowering Vision for Congregations is Not About Me

God does not necessarily want your congregation to be successful, to grow big, to compete with other churches, to be the church with the best reputation, the most beautiful buildings, the friendliest people, the most outstanding preacher, significant missional engagement, or to be the best at reaching young adult families.

That is, unless any of these is God's empowering vision for your congregation. God much prefers for you to be a congregation that lives into its God-given vision rather than a congregation who sets its goals and then asks God to bless them.

For congregations captured by God's empowering vision it is all about God rather than about the congregation. It is not about "me" where "me" is the congregation. It is not about having the same vision as the congregation down the street. It is not about unanimous congregational support for God's empowering vision. It is not about a journey with an end where congregations can declare they are finished.

Here are some *Vision Insights* that speak to my perspective on congregations, God's role in vision, and the "me" factor.

Vision Insight 012: The word vision contains neither the letter "m" nor the letter "e." Vision is not about "me." It is about God.

Vision is about God and what God desires to do in and through "me." It is about what God desires to do in and through your congregation.

We should never boast that we have a vision, or that we are successfully fulfilling that vision. We should always boast in the Lord, and thank God for all that is happening within and around us as we work to fulfill God's empowering vision for our congregation.

"Look at me and what I have done," is always an indicator leaders have not truly been captured by God's empowering vision, but desire people to agree with their vision.

Vision Insight 013: Do not confuse our eternal mission, your everlasting purpose, and your enduring core values with God's empowering vision.

These are distinctive aspects of the spiritual and strategy journey of a congregation. Our eternal mission is God's mission that we most commonly know through the Great Commission and the Great Commandment. Mark 16:15 and Mark 12:22, coupled with Luke 4:18-19 are for many people the best biblical representations of the Commission and the Commandment of God.

Congregations sometimes use "mission" as the branding statement that expresses their generic understanding of what a Christian congregation should be doing. One example is a congregation with whom I consulted who branded what they did as "Loving God, Loving People, and Loving the World." There was nothing specific and contextual about this mission statement. It simply branded their identity and annual program of ministry.

Purpose speaks to the historic reason why a given congregation was launched in a particular location among a particular group of people. Enduring core values speak into key theological, ethical, and cultural values that are closely held by a congregation.

- **Words and Ideas:** Check out additional characteristics of planning language that involves "mission," "purpose," "core values." and "vision."

Vision Insight 014: Vision is specific to your congregation. Mission is transferable to many congregations in your denominational family.

A key difference between mission and vision is that God's mission, although powerful and sure, is general in the sense that it is applicable to every congregation. All Christianity seeks to faithfully fulfill the same mission of God.

Vision, however, must be specifically stated or clearly implied in terms that are unique to each congregation. What is it that God is calling your congregation to be and do over the next seven years? How would you share and illustrate vision keeping in mind the context where God has placed you?

Vision Insight 015: Even if only a small percentage of leaders in your congregation are visionaries, God still has a perfect vision for you.

Having vision does not depend on many visionaries being present in your congregation. Of course, the more visionaries you have the more likely you are to be captured by and living into vision.

We know from decades of work that if at least seven percent of the active, attending congregation is captured by God's empowering vision for the congregation there is a greater chance vision will be embraced by the congregation.

- **Words and Ideas:** What is the meaning of "seven percent" and how does it relate to the "21 percent?"

Vision Insight 016: Vision is about pressing on towards the prize of the high calling of God in Christ Jesus as shared in Philippians 3:14.

A spiritual and strategic journey is like a race we are running at the speed of God's leadership and our discernment of God's vision. Often vision comes not all at once. It is likely felt and experienced over a defined period. It sharpens, and even partially changes its focus from time-to-time.

Therefore, congregations cannot say they have arrived, completed, or fulfilled their vision. It is a spiritual and strategic journey. It does not have a finite distance. It can have an infinite impact.

With God as Our Source Congregational Vision is More Than Numbers

Let's be certain about vision. It is not easy. The clear majority of pastors, staff persons, and lay leaders have a difficult time understanding vision. It is not second nature to them. Their vision may be something they can see, whereas God's empowering vision is unseen and we arrive at it by faith.

Leaders—even in Christian congregations—may approach vision as if a church is an organization, a sports team, or their country. It is about winning. It is about reaching tangible goals in the short-term. They cannot separate the success they see in the world around them from the success only God can offer.

To many congregations this translates as a numerical measurement. Vision is a growing membership and attendance. Vision is program events that are wildly successful. Vision is surpassing the budget. Vision is filling the worship center. Vision is a full schedule of ministries.

The source of these visions is our own pride.

With God as our source a whole different measuring standard for success is utilized. It is more about seeing God as the source and allowing God to define our success. To do this we must exhibit a deep relationship with God. Vision fulfillment may result in numerical growth, Yet, it is the fulfillment of vision that should be the core focus.

For example, if God's empowering vision is to reach residents of your transitioning neighborhood, or to offer your seldom used gymnasium to local clubs and that makes some members uncomfortable, then they may leave. Fulfilling that vision may not result in numerical growth.

In some congregational cultures, God's empowering vision and church growth are inseparable. I agree God wants congregations to be faithful, effective, and innovative in connecting people with the Triune God. I agree the Good News is not only for everyone, but needed by everyone. I pray all might be believers in and followers of Jesus, the living Word of God.

But, to make numbers the primary divining rod concerning the rightness and goodness of vision is to marginalize the full richness of what God can do in and thorough congregations. I further agree that if congregations with faithfulness, effectiveness, and innovation live into God's empowering vision for them that it is inevitable that directly or indirectly through their ministry Kingdom growth will take place, and this will include an increase in numbers.

Here are some *Vision Insights* that speak to my perspective on congregations and God as the source of vision.

Vision Insight 017: When congregations are in the best possible relationship with God and one another they can easily experience vision.

Distance from God in the spiritual walk of leaders and the congregation is a key aspect of the ease or difficulty of acquiring vision, plus the depth and passion surrounding vision. Leaders and congregations who walk closely and are at one with the Triune God are more easily captured by vision and passionate about its fulfillment.

Leaders and congregations with a shallow, distant relationship with the Triune God have a more difficult time being captured by vision and caring about its fulfillment. Relational distance from God makes vision hard to feel and hard to establish.

Vision Insight 018: Vision is not a passing fantasy or a fleeting passion. It is a long-term view of God's calling on a congregation.

Vision is not about quick results. Its fulfillment does not have to be fast. It is a commitment over a long period. Vision is not about what we will do this budget year. That is focusing on tactics. Vision is not about the next one to three years. That is focusing on strategies. Vision is about the long-term.

Vision is about changed behavior that develops over years, and becomes hardwired in the Christ-centered, faith-based culture of the congregation. It is about being part of a congregation that is on a long-distance journey with which people desire to be connected.

Vision Insight 019: Earthly things, preferences, and tangible security blind us to the brilliance of God's new vision.

Humankind regularly confuses the leadership of God, the culture of the congregations they have known, and their patriotism regarding their country. This confusion can be sufficiently strong that culture and patriotism are more intensely expressed than God's leadership regarding the spiritual and strategic vision and direction of congregations.

The earthly success of congregations too often becomes more important than both the significance of the missional service and the surrender to God's empowering vision. This leads to opposition unless change is good for the culture or good for patriotism. Congregations should look to God's empowering vision to define and frame their change.

Vision Insight 020: God offers transformative vision. Too often our possessions, deference to other people, and pride blind us as we are only open to transactional vision.

To be captured by God's empowering vision is a paradigm shift. When such a shift occurs then everything goes back to zero. The transformative vision God offers congregations requires the re-evaluation of everything congregations do in light of the new vision.

When our church buildings, our unwillingness to take a stand for where God is leading us, and the pride we feel in our heritage conflict with God's transformative vision, too many congregations reject God's empowering vision. They want change they can see and immediately measure. That is a transactional vision. God's transformational vision is unseen and long-term.

Key Points for Your Congregation

First, it is not about God blessing your vision, it is about God's empowering vision being a blessing to your congregation and its involvement in the mission of God.

Second, only God's empowering vision will be sufficient for your congregation. The vision of the pastor, a staff person, a long-term member, a new member, the governance leaders, the ministry leaders, nor the people with the greatest passion about the future of the congregation is sufficient. Only God's empowering vision will suffice.

Third, the specific vision God has for your congregation for the next stage of its life is not defined by the overarching mission of any Christian congregation. Vision is specific, timely, and contextual to your congregation.

Fourth, vision is not about temporal things like numbers and growth. These may be the result of living into God's empowering vision. Vision is more about being in the center of God's will for your congregation.

Call to Action for Your Congregation

Dialogue with a small group of diverse participants in your congregation around God's role in vision. If God is truly the source of vision for your congregation, and you have always thought the pastor, staff, or key lay leaders ought to provide it, how does this chapter change your perspective on vision? On leadership? On the role of the pastor? On your dependence on God?

Consider what you have always thought was the content of vision. Numerical growth? New or renovated buildings? A larger staff? The success of programs? If these are not the signs of vision fulfillment, then what are the signs? Pray for a deeper willingness for God to be the source of vision, and what that means about your responsibility to be part of a community of people—a congregation—with vision.

A Prayer for Your Congregation

God of grace and God of glory, may we clearly see You as the source of vision. May we engage in deep and meaningful dialogue and prayer to discern Your vision for our congregation. May we clearly understand vision is not about asking You to bless our vision, but asking that we may be a blessing to You as we live into Your vision for our congregation. May we resist attempts to allow the vision of humankind to blur Your vision for us. For Your glory we yearn. Amen.

CHAPTER THREE

Pastors and the Enduring Visionary Leadership Community

Vision casting is everyone's responsibility

St. Paul's Church had been through a decade long, unintentional ensmallment campaign that resulted in attendance dropping by half within ten years. Resulting financial constraints forced them to drastically reduce staff. For a year, they went through a slow healing process, and finally arrived at a place where they could begin to think about their future.

Although they wanted to engage in a visioning process the pastor felt staff was overloaded due to the downsizing. They could not lead such a process even with the assistance of an outside strategic leadership coach.

The pastor challenged his lay leaders to take responsibility to engage in a visioning process looking toward the next ten years. They needed to set a new direction. They needed assurance of God's empowering vision for their future.

A dedicated laywoman volunteered to lead the process, and the congregation followed her on a journey that was both spiritual and strategic. Their year-long process took them to a place from which they could be captured by God's new vision for them.

What they found is that their passionate lay leadership, along with the pastor and staff, coalesced into what I identify as an *Enduring Visionary Leadership Community*. They were willing to follow God's lead to new heights, take new risks, and call on laypersons for focused involvement.

This new excitement and commitment led them to focus their future ministry around a dozen lay-led teams coached by the pastor and key staff. The staff was reconceptualized from functioning primarily as program directors to focusing their time on serving as team coaches. This moved them far away from a pattern where the pastor is expected to be the source of vision, originate a visionary movement, and to keep pushing it along.

Congregations put high pressure on their senior or solo pastor to originate vision. They want a new pastor to bring vision. This highlights confusion between God's role in vision, as mentioned in the previous chapter, and the pastor's role in vision. This is a common challenge for virtually every congregation.

How often does a congregation that begins to feel the pastor is not bringing vision, or cannot sell a vision, replace the pastor? Too often. Culture bound, they feel "If the team ain't winnin' it's time to fire the coach."

All this rhetoric misses the point. While pastors are a key to visionary leadership, they are not the source of congregational vision. A lay leadership community also has a crucial role in vision. Five simply stated keys are foundational.

The Five Keys to Visionary Leadership

1. **Senior or Solo Pastor:** The senior or solo pastor is, indeed, the first among the five keys. It is important for pastors to acknowledge they do have a role and responsibility in vision casting. Yet vision may not come easy to them. I've found as many as 80 percent of all pastors do not find vision casting an easy task. I have heard others suggest this percentage is higher.
2. **Lay Leaders:** There must be a set of visionary lay leaders within the life of the congregation supported by the pastor and staff

persons. At least seven percent of the average number of adults present during a typical weekend for worship must participate in vision casting and be captured by vision.

3. **God's Empowering Vision:** There must be a clearly discerned vision for the future of the congregation. Where there is no vision the congregation will perish, to paraphrase Proverbs 29:18. A God-given vision must be part of the fabric of the congregation.

4. **Reasonable Resources:** There must be reasonable resources to support strategic programming, ministries, and activities, and to align them for the fulfillment of the vision. Congregations cannot make brick without straw just as the Israelite people could not in Egypt. Reasonable resources must be present or acquired to empower the vision to come alive.

5. **God's Timing:** There must be a clear sense of God's timing. Visionary leadership does not happen because the calendar says it is time for a new or renewed vision, because a meeting is called to determine vision, or because a committee is appointed to develop a vision. Vision happens when there is a movement of God that creates memorable visionary experiences.

With this foundation, let's return to the role of pastor as one of the keys to visionary leadership.

The Pastor is the Voice of Vision

While the senior or solo pastor has a key role as the voice of vision, the Triune God is the originator or source of vision. The pastor should be among the first persons, if not the very first person to be captured by God's empowering vision for the future of the congregation.

However, the senior or solo pastor alone does not bring forth vision. It is the pastor plus staff and lay leaders equal to seven percent of the average number of people present during a typical weekend for worship within the congregation. This number includes the pastor, staff, and people with positive spiritual passion about the future of the church to which God is calling the congregation.

To be fully effective, these seven percent must be supported by another 14 percent who are people of various positions within the life and ministry of the congregation. This adds up to a number equal to 21 percent of attendees, and is an informal congregational leadership community or guiding coalition called the *Enduring Visionary Leadership Community.*

If it is the senior or solo pastor's vision alone then it comes and goes as the pastor comes and goes. In these cases, the congregation seldom develops deep ownership. In this model the pastor has the tough task of always pushing the congregation to understand and live into his or her vision.

Pushing may work in the short-term. But only being pulled forward by a prophetic understanding of God's empowering vision will bring success, significance, and surrender to the congregation.

Pastors Leave Congregations but God's Empowering Vision Never Leaves

When a congregation expects the next pastor to bring them vision, that implies that vision comes from the pastor.

It also implies the last pastor did not have a vision for the congregation. Further, it implies vision comes and goes with pastors, and is not always present. How do you feel about these understandings?

If vision is from God and is not present for a congregation, then is God's empowering vision for a congregation temporary, and comes and goes? If so, that says God does not always have a vision for a congregation.

I believe God has a perfect vision for all congregations for all times. The challenge is that congregations too often do not connect with God's empowering vision for them. Or, they allow the vision to wane.

This leads to several *Vision Insights* that are important for congregations to consider about God, vision, and pastors.

Vision Insight 021: Visionary Leadership is about who we are, what we believe, where we are headed, and how we are getting there.

In one sense this is a restatement of mission, purpose, core values, vision, and the alignment of congregational actions to live into or fulfill the vision. It asks the question, "Do we know who we are in relationship to the Triune God, why we were founded as a congregation, what we value or believe, where we are headed, and how we are going to get there?"

Vision Insight 022: Vision plus Intentionality is the core formula for an *Enduring Visionary Leadership Community* to follow.

Congregations seeking to transform only need three words to describe the essence of a transformation strategy. Vision. Plus. Intentionality. If the deep meaning of these three words captivates the imagination of at least 21 percent of the average number of active attending adults, then it is likely the congregation has vision. These 21 percent are the *Enduring Visionary Leadership Community*.

Vision Insight 023: If congregations focus on the pastor's vision, when the pastor leaves vision often leaves. Vision from God never leaves.

Does your congregation want a temporal vision or an eternal vision? For many people that is an easy question. Of course, they want an eternal vision. If so, then why do they expect the pastor, staff, and key lay leaders to provide it? Any vision of humankind is going to be temporal. It comes and goes as the fads and trends change. It focuses the congregation on short-term fixes rather than long-term solutions.

God's empowering vision never leaves. It may wane within a congregation and need re-invigorating, but it never leaves.

Vision Insight 024: If vision is deeply felt throughout the congregation, it does not diminish when there is a transition in pastors.

This is a key reason why congregations should never want the vision they are following to be the pastor's vision. That is a lot of power and authority to give a pastor. When the vision is primarily the pastor's, the congregation seldom owns it.

If a congregation is captured by God's empowering vision, deeply feels ownership, faithfully, effectively, and with innovation lives into it, then when a pastor leaves vision remains. Rather than diminishing, it may flourish as any existing staff plus lay leaders come forward to work more fervently on vision fulfillment.

Vision Insight 025: When congregations expect the pastor to provide vision, they often mean a vision with which they agree.

Even if a congregation is sold on or blind to anything except the pastor being the CVO (chief visionary officer), CCO (chief casting officer), and CIO (chief implementation officer), they often mean the content of the vision and the action to fulfill it must meet criteria that is typically unknown to the pastor. What laity mean is that vision must fit the unspoken culture of the congregation.

The congregation may have a set of hidden core values. They are well known to the long tenured members, only slightly known to the short tenured members, and possibly totally unknown to a new pastor who comes in excited to lead the vision he or she has for the congregation.

Excellence Eludes Pastors Not Passionate About Vision

Early in my ministry I served on the national missions staff of my denomination. Those were wonderful years. I served with a group of highly committed ministers with a deep passion for helping leaders, congregations, and regional denominational organizations reach their full Kingdom potential. It was hard work. I traveled nationally at a time I had two preschool children.

About the time I adjusted to the travel, and my wife and I figured out how to create high quality family life amid my schedule, I was called to a regional denominational position in my wife's home state. In many ways, we saw this as a reward after four years of a challenging schedule. Most of my travel would now be day trips.

Unfortunately, we realized the depth of passion and commitment to excellence we experienced in the national missions agency did not exist in this state. Elements we considered mediocre at the national agency were seen as excellence in this regional denomination.

It took a while to figure out the issue was vision. At the national agency, we saw clear vision and deep passion around the overall mission of God. In the regional denomination we experienced a culture of "good enough is good enough." We will come back to this story later, and refer to excellence versus mediocrity.

For now, my point is that this is not unlike the experience in local congregations when laypersons, staff, and pastor, are not passionate about God's empowering vision for their congregation. Here are several *Vision Insights* that speak into passion, vision, and pastors.

Vision Insight 026: Pastors not passionate about God's empowering vision for their congregation are likely to gain a reputation as mediocre.

Let's admit it. From everything we know fewer than 20 percent of all pastors are true visionaries with a deep passion surrounding what will characterize their congregation if they live into the call of God upon them.

Without an awareness of vision from God for their congregation, pastors will do more wandering around than moving forward. Their ministry and reputation will be mediocre. They may be nice persons, as one called into Christian ministry, but also as one without sharp and decisive spiritual gifts surrounding leadership.

They may love their congregation, and their congregation may love them. The congregation may call them effective, but that will generally be because even the congregation sees mediocrity as excellence.

Vision Insight 027: Pastors not passionate about God's empowering vision for their congregation are likely to become known as "former pastor."

If there is a mismatch between what the congregation expects in leadership from the pastor, and the pastor's performance in that area, then "former pastor" may be his or her new title.

This issue is substantially different than situations where congregations expect their pastor to bring vision and push it out to the congregation. This is about congregations where there is a true, deep, and genuine desire for God's empowering vision, but they need their pastor to lead them to embrace it by being the CCO (chief casting officer).

Either the pastor refuses or the pastor is among the 80 percent or more of pastors who do not get it about vision and their role in casting it. Vision casting is not taught in many seminaries, and it does not come naturally to many pastors.

Vision Insight 028: Pastors and staff who feel entitled to their role with a particular congregation are not likely to empower vision.

Entitlement is dicey. Different things are seen in different situations as comprising entitlement. An entitlement mentality is more prolific than many people acknowledge.

Entitlement is present among both laypersons and clergy. When pastors and church staff persons develop an entitlement mentality about their role they defend it, fight for it, and resist any change in it.

If pastors and staff feel entitled to their job, and believe nothing can take it away from them, they have little urgency to help cast and fulfill passionate, empowering vision for the future of their congregation. Consequently, they suffer, the congregation suffers, and a small part of God's Kingdom suffers.

Vision Casting is the Responsibility of All Congregational Leaders

Matt Carswell is an example of a gifted preacher, and a warm, caring pastor. He excels in spiritual formation through worship and in-depth pastoral care. His congregation loves him.

At the same time, when it comes to leading forward progress for his congregation he is lost. Casting vision, then aligning the programs, ministries, and activities of the congregation around vision is not one of his strengths. He understands its importance. He just cannot do it.

Because he understands he must provide visionary leadership, he seeks to discover staff persons and lay leaders for whom vision comes naturally, and coaches them in the process of vision plus intentional actions to live into that vision. He also allows them to coach him in casting vision through preaching, teaching, and personal influence.

Vision casting needs to be the responsibility of all congregational leaders. The best visions are ones where the senior or solo pastor is not the only vision casting person.

Vision Insight 029: When pastors do not get vision easily, they may find some true visionaries among their congregation who do get it.

If we can get beyond the false idea that pastors bring vision, and all pastors are visionary leaders, we may be able to address vision from a healthier perspective. Since a key principle is that God is seeking to impart vision to the whole congregation, then many pastors need to listen and discern what God is saying to the congregation.

They need to identify people who are visionaries, then pray, dialogue, and plan with them. A wise pastor does not have to have all the answers, but can nurture and benefit from the various spiritual gifts present among people within the congregation.

Wise pastors like Matt Carswell will discover people within their congregation who do understand vision and how it applies in Christian congregations as an organism in motion. The pastor may recruit these people as a team to initiate an envisioning process, and then coach them in their task. This way the pastor is part of the visionary leadership, and does not need to feel guilty about struggling with the concept of vision, how to discern it, and how to cast it.

It is a significant dilemma when the senior or solo pastor does not get it about vision, and one or more staff persons, plus some laity do get it. It creates a real crisis in many congregations. This crisis can escalate if the pastor is in denial about vision and opposes approaches for dialogue from staff persons and lay leaders.

Vision Insight 030: Vision casting is the responsibility of all leaders in a congregation with the pastor providing initiating leadership.

Pastors would do well to distinguish between directive leadership and initiating leadership. Directive leadership is straight-forward leadership based on the principles and perspectives of the leader. Initiating leadership seeks to start and coach the essential processes of a congregation.

Vision casting is more about initiating leadership than directive leadership. Initiating leaders may be better at vision casting than those who are directive leaders. Initiating leaders can be artistic and inclusive in vision casting. Directive leaders may believe it is all about them.

Vision Insight 031: Few followers get vision easily. Leaders must paint a picture of what the congregation could be like once captured by vision.

A key part of a pastor's vision casting role is using preaching, teaching, and other formal and informal opportunities to tell stories and paint a vivid picture of what vision looks, feels, and acts like within the congregation and its community context.

They need to talk about Genesis 12 and the journey of Abram's clan, or the Exodus being led by the cloud by day and fire by night, or the vision of Paul from God to come over to Macedonia, or Peter realizing the Good News is for everyone so he needs to go to the Gentiles, or many other stories from the Bible where God led people towards something not yet seen.

Vision Insight 032: Potential leaders who cannot articulate their passion for the congregation's vision need to remain "potential leaders."

The functioning of lay leaders regarding vision needs to focus around their passion for fulfilling vision. If current and potential lay leaders do not feel passion for the vision and for fulfilling it, their actions and attitudes will not inspire anyone else to see and follow.

Too many lay leaders have their own agenda. Once they are in a leadership position they seek to push their vision rather than to be part of God's empowering vision. No matter how competent these potential leaders are, how powerful they are, and even how much money they give, their presence in crucial leadership positions can derail God's empowering vision for the congregation.

Other potential leaders have no understanding of vision or of the need to move their congregations beyond ministry as usual. They don't need to be super persons, faster than a speeding bullet, more powerful than a locomotive, and able to leap tall buildings in a single bound. They do need to aspire to a desire for their congregation to be a super church.

Vision Insight 033: Casting vision is a forever activity. When does congregational leadership finish casting vision? Never, or vision wanes.

Pastors, staff members, and lay leaders must continually cast vision until it becomes second nature. In casting vision, they are not promoting something to the congregation. They are celebrating a current and emerging characteristic of their congregation.

Casting vision is like spouses telling one another of their mutual love. Making that declaration is never finished and is never trite. Expressing love reminds spouses why they truly love, and celebrates their lifelong relationship.

Your members need to be in love with the Triune God, just as the Triune God is in love with all persons. Congregations need to love living into God's empowering vision for them. They need to continually cast vision, and allow it to roll effortlessly off their tongues.

Organizational Leaders Should Leave Their Ideas About Congregational Vision at the Office

Many congregations have within their membership successful and insightful business and organizational leaders who daily make a significant impact in the marketplace. Some are entrepreneurs who started their own businesses, or assumed leadership of a family business they saw developing as they grew up in the home of an entrepreneur. Others have risen within the ranks of an already well established organization and learned proven success principles.

Regardless of their pathway, these leaders can contribute much to their congregations. Congregations should make use of sound business principles in the way they develop their spiritual and strategic journey. Too few do. Some do not do this because they believe business principles have no place in a congregation.

Others do not do this because the pastor, staff, and influential key leaders are clueless about sound organizational principles. They do not realize that if their congregation was a for-profit business it might have to declare bankruptcy to survive.

Business principles can organize congregations for efficiency and effectiveness in fulfilling the mission of God. For example, businesses that do it right can teach congregations about customer service that can be applied to congregational efforts to assimilate new people.

The downside of introducing business principles into congregations is that too often they can be the wrong principles with the wrong mindset and the wrong outcomes.

Business principles come from a secular organizational framework—with few exceptions. Congregations have a spiritual organism framework—we hope. Way too many cultural enclaves seek to pass themselves off as Christian congregations.

Organizational and organism frameworks do not mix. They are oil and water. Too often neither the business layperson nor the clergy understand where they are missing one another in this dialogue. They just know they are in conflict over how to run the church.

This is particularly true when it comes to congregational vision, which as stated earlier is a movement that is memorable rather than a statement that is memorized. Statements are for organizations. Movements are for organisms. Here is a *Vision Insight* that speaks to this perspective.

Vision Insight 034: Vision crafted using an organizational model misses the fact that a congregation is a spiritual organism.

Vision in an organization comes from the passion and dreams of leaders. They work hard to push their organization forward to achieve success. Even with the best of apparent altruism, the goal is the success of the organization.

Obviously, the philanthropy of some organizations, and some of their leaders, moves into the realm of significance. However, success remains the primary goal. Any movement toward significance often follows the achievement of success.

Vision in a spiritual organism comes from God. The desire of congregations is to allow God to pull them forward to achieve significance and ultimately full surrender to God's leadership. As spiritual organisms, congregations are movements of people rather than the production and sale of products and services.

Significance should be a priority for congregations, and should be pursued first. The hope is that success will follow so the congregation is sustainable and can achieve a mindset, attitude, and quality of surrender to God's will.

An organizational model focuses congregational efforts on accountable management and is flavored by programs or service oriented-efforts. Budgets are met. Costs are held down. Staff positions are few. Programs are successful. The congregation is growing in numbers as a byproduct of quality.

A spiritual organism model focuses on visionary leadership and relationship experiences which express themselves through spiritual formation, leadership development, and missional engagement. Congregations mature in the quality of the fulfillment of their vision, and may also be growing in numbers.

Therefore, let business leaders leave their ideas about congregational vision at the office. Let them empower the process of vision within their congregation. Perhaps they are to take the process of vision with them from their congregation to their office to enhance the quality of their secular work.

Key Points for Your Congregation

First, vision is not the responsibility of just the pastor. All leaders and all other willing persons must seek to discern God's empowering vision for their congregation. At the same time, recognize the pastor does have a responsibility of being the voice of vision.

Second, if the vision is owned only by the pastor, then it does not reside in the heart, soul, mind and strength of the congregation. This means when the pastor is gone, the vision is likely gone.

Third, always remember congregations are not organizations. They are organisms. As such, organizational principles that come strictly from the business world seldom fit congregations captured by God's empowering vision. Day-to-day good organizational principles should be present in a congregation. Year-to-year the values of a spiritual organism should guide the pathway of a congregation.

Call to Action for Your Congregation

Expect, encourage, and support the pastor, staff, and key lay leaders as an *Enduring Visionary Leadership Community* as they seek to cast the vision God is inspiring within the life and ministry of the congregation. Give feedback as to the clarity with which they are casting vision, the passion you feel about the vision, and your willingness to help in fulfilling the vision.

A Prayer for Your Congregation

O Lord, may vision within our congregation and the communities of people we serve who are near and far, be the light that illuminates the darkness, the cloud that goes before us by day as well as the fire that goes before us at night, and excites within our souls the glory of the all-consuming fire of Elijah at Mount Carmel. With a burning desire to daily experience the light of the world, we pray. Amen.

CHAPTER FOUR

Vision—Written or Experienced?

Which comes first: a statement or an experience?

After several years of things just not going right in their church, Taylor
Road called a new pastor. While they had been healing for a while, the
new pastor was quickly aware they needed more healing to develop a strong
foundation for envisioning the next season of their life.

To a certain degree this was a risk. The new pastor had been urged by
the pastor selection team to come in the door casting new vision. He had
a reputation for fast starts in every congregation he served. The team
wanted a fast start. But as often happens, the new pastor realized the pastor
selection team was farther along in their healing than the congregation.

Two years into his tenure, and after starting a second worship service
that had a contemporary style, the pastor perceived they were ready. He
engaged a strategic leadership coach to help the congregation envision its
next season.

He knew they needed a sense of forward movement more than a written
vision statement. Ultimately they would need a clear statement. They
found it by discerning a narrative future story that told what they would
be like ten years into the future if they with faithfulness, effectiveness, and
innovation lived into God's call for them.

The amazing thing that happened, however, is that during the year of becoming captured by God's empowering vision their attendance increased 25 percent. Results did not wait for the process to be completed because members began displaying a new spirit of vision and people responded.

Guests noticed an inviting attitude once members previously entrenched in long-term programs realized they needed to let go of their control and allow God to do a new thing in their midst. Creative dialogue began taking place about a series of small group gatherings to help people grow spiritually and to engage people outside the congregation in faith-based dialogue.

What happened is that vision was not first written. It was first experienced. The congregation had become ready like a race car at the starting line, revved up, slamming into gear and hitting the track at full throttle.

Is Congregational Vision Written Then Experienced or Experienced Then Written?

Is a vision best when written or best when experienced? Yes, and it depends. But, let's go deeper.

Think about your dreams last night. Yes, you dreamed, but you may not remember them. If you do remember did you dream in pictures or words? Did you interact with people or a script you were reading? Did you dream in color or black and white?

Of course your dreams were pictures, experiences, and interactions. It was not a script. First you see pictures or metaphors. Often you interact with people in pleasant or unpleasant ways, but you are not reading a script.

Dreams and visions are cousins. When you imagine a vision, is it words or a statement you are imagining? Or, is it an experience or a picture of a destination? Is it a metaphor of some type that represents your vision? Is God in your dreams?

A recent congregational client expressed their vision using the metaphor of a pizza. The crust, the sauce, and the cheese each meant something of significance about their future story that represented their vision. It was important that people saw the metaphor before they ever saw the words of the future story. In this case, they could almost smell and taste vision.

Generally, the very best visions are experienced first, and then at some point when they mature they are written down for sharing. I believe how the New Testament came to us is one way to look at the coming of vision and whether it is written or experienced.

Cecil B. DeMille, that legendary American filmmaker best known for the *Ten Commandments* released in 1956, and a group of screenwriters got in a back room and wrote a screenplay. Then they handed it to Jesus and the Apostles with the instructions "Say and do this!" Yeah. Right.

The New Testament, especially the gospels, were experienced, the stories were told and retold. Then when a written record was needed for accuracy and to reach people and churches to which the Apostles could not travel, it was written. Vision is best experienced first, and later written for clarity and sharing.

Also, many statements that are called vision are very general, generic statements that are better called "mission." Or, they might be considered a motto, or a branding statement if you're talking about marketing. Any written vision statement needs to be experienced as unique for your congregation.

Here are two *Vision Insights* that focus about a written vision statement versus vision being experienced.

Vision Insight 035: Any similarity between the typical committee-developed vision statement and true vision is purely accidental.

Committees write statements, create mottos, and too often emulate something they have heard or seen elsewhere. They also confuse vision with mission which is easy to do as the word "mission" has so many meanings and applications.

Committee-developed visions are often words rather than experiences, pictures, or metaphors. The words may represent a negotiated compromise around which everyone feels good. Seldom do the words sharply captivate the passion of many people in the congregation.

Even if well-crafted, a vision statement belongs primarily to the crafters and must be sold to the congregation for there to be any reasonable depth of ownership

Some of the best vision statements are developed by congregational participants as their personal elevator speech to convey the spiritual and strategic direction of the congregation. If their elevator speech is compatible with the general understanding—even the wording—of their congregational vision it is perfect for them to use.

Vision Insight 036: Vision is not so much written as it is experienced. Vision must be sensed and experienced more than read or heard.

Vision must naturally flows out of as many congregational participants as possible as they give their full heart, soul, mind, and strength to the vision as one part of the journey to fulfill the overall mission of God.

Yes, we eventually need vision in a written form as a personal reminder. And, yes, we need it in written form to share with others and to create a consistent message. It is even all right to memorize it.

More than all of this we need to experience vision in our own lives and ministries as Christian individuals and as congregations. We must be able to talk about vision as a feeling and not just a thought. It must be a personalized story more than a written statement.

The order of experience to written is important. Continue to think about the idea of order as you read the next section.

George W. Bullard Jr.

Just Like the New Testament, Congregational Vision is Experienced Then Written

Who knows for sure exactly how the gospel of Luke was written? I mean exactly. No one knows with absolute assurance. But, we can imagine.

To ignite my imagination, I read the first four verses of Luke and discovered some interesting things. First, the author did research. He compiled an account of the things that had happened. Second, he did not compile just random things, but those things "on which there was full conviction." (See the note for Luke 1:1 in NASB.)

Third, his sources were the oral tradition—and perhaps some early writings—of those who were eyewitnesses to the events of the life of Jesus. Fourth, he investigated carefully everything that was available to him from the beginning. Fifth, to the best of his knowledge, he sought to place things in chronological order.

Sixth, he wanted Theophilus as a representative of those who would read this Gospel to know as truthfully as possible the things on which he had been "orally instructed. (See the note for Luke 1:4 in NASB.) During this holy experience of writing, certainly he felt the inspiration of the Triune God.

In the same manner, congregations who become captured by God's empowering vision should ultimately put into words their experiences of vision, and the oral tradition that develops around congregational vision.

Here are four *Vision Insights* that focus on writing a congregational vision.

Vision Insight 037: When considering how vision comes to us, it may be helpful to consider how the New Testament came to us. It came by experience first, and then was recorded.

The New Testament—particularly the four gospels—did not come to us as a movie screenplay or television mini-series. The New Testament did not come to us first as a written story.

The New Testament came to us as a real-life experience from an oral tradition culture which told and retold the stories of Jesus they had experienced in life. At a certain point when those who personally had interacted with Jesus could not be everywhere the stories were collected, preserved, validated, authenticated—and written down.

Obviously they went through various editions until they wound up in the canon of our New Testament.

Vision Insight 038: Vision is experienced. We reflect on it and share it orally with our full heart, soul, mind, and strength. Then we write it.

Vision should be first experienced, and the stories and concepts about it allowed to mature, before we canonize a statement. Life experiences before words about life experiences are essential. *I-Thou* before *I-It* in the tradition of Jewish theologian Martin Buber, as referred to in chapter one, is a great perspective on this. (See Vision Insight 006.)

What are the stories of vision in your congregation that have been told repeatedly that you now need to record? If you have a vision statement, do these stories accurately illustrate the vision? Does it need to be updated in any way to reflect God's current movement in your congregation?

Vision Insight 039: We write the vision we have experienced to create a consistent historic and dynamic record of the vision to share with the congregation and others.

When writing your statement of vision use clear and decisive words that fit the culture of the congregation and its community context. You want people who read it to say, "Yes, this is it!"

They also should think of an experiential story of their own that fits with the statement. They may also develop their own paraphrased interpretation that fits into their congregational vision experience.

Some years ago, I helped a large regional denomination develop a new visionary movement for its service with congregations. It was called

Empowering Kingdom Growth. We waited a while to write a statement that communicated our vision. Eventually we said it was time to put it in words to communicate with our affiliated congregations. A few months later we revised it slightly to more clearly state our intent and passion. After that it remained untouched for seven years.

Vision Insight 040: Since vision is not a statement, do not try borrowing a vision statement from your favorite congregation.

Sure, I have my favorites. But I try not to impose my language on a congregation that I'm helping. Besides, when a congregation pilfers the language of another congregation they're often picking up the mission statement, motto or tagline and not actually their vision statement.

I like what Shawn Lovejoy says in his book on congregational vision entitled *Be Mean About Vision: Preserving and Protecting What Matters* (Thomas Nelson, 2016). On page 20 he says, "Don't rip off someone else's vision. God has something better—much more authentic—that's meant just for you."

That is so true for every congregation I encounter. The best visions are the ones that fit each congregation perfectly. Do not borrow. Be unique. Be who God is calling you to be.

Should Congregations Stay Away from Professionals When Writing a Vision Statement?

Yes, and for very good reasons. There is nothing wrong with professionals, but congregations develop a dependency on outside third parties who help them craft their future vision. Because ownership is such an important part of any vision statement, and because it needs to be something that emerges out of members' passionate experience, to use a professional marketer or strategist to craft the vision statement does not enhance its value.

What a professional marketing strategist can do well is help you polish the statement once crafted. They can help you align the vision statement with other things you are writing, sharing, and communicating. They can help you evaluate whether the things you are doing to fulfill your vision connect with the vision statement.

It is always possible a coaching relationship can assist you while you are writing your vision statement. This should be a process coaching relationship of discovery and not one where the coach provides you with actual content other than as an example of multiple ways your vision statement could be crafted.

"The counterpoint is that vision must connect with people who may not have the same depth of God talk in their lifestyle as the deeply committed disciples who form the people of passion in congregations," said my friend, John Bost, of Winston-Salem, NC.

Here are three *Vision Insights* that focus on the authentic nature of a written vision statement versus a professional vision statement.

Vision Insight 041: Too much focus on a professionally crafted vision statement takes the focus off a real visionary experience.

While your vision statement must communicate clearly, it should not be so polished and sterile that it does not speak into the actual experience of the congregation. Have a marketing strategy for its context, but overly polishing your vision statement to use as a marketing tool often distracts from the power and passion around a vision.

It is not the well-crafted and professionally polished vision statement that is likely to increase the invitational quality of a congregation. It is the relationship with people, and the meaning and significance of the visionary experience in the life and ministry of the congregation that will entice others.

Stories about real visionary experiences that speak into the lives of others are the most powerful marketing tools. Yes, a professional marketing strategist can assist you in realizing when you have some great stories, but they do not originate them. The stories must be the real experiences of real people connected with your congregation who are willing to engage others through their storytelling.

Vision Insight 042: Vision is not about doing the same old things the same old ways and giving them a new name and motto.

Vision is not window dressing. It is not just style. It is substantive, real, new, and innovative content, focus, and direction. It is not dressing up what you have been doing for many years and calling it a new vision from God. That focuses on the past. Vision always focuses on the future towards which God is pulling the congregation.

It is not that the same old things done in the same old ways were wrong or bad. They just highlight the past over the future. While the core substance and spiritual foundation of the gospel proclaimed from the first century forward never changes, the strategies and structures for nurturing and proclaiming the gospel message modulate over time. The style with which the gospel message is proclaimed is in constant flux.

I once heard legendary Christian speaker and writer Len Sweet say he had changed his style of preaching five times during his ministry in response to the changing patterns of succeeding generations of followers of Jesus. Read carefully. These were changes in style, not in the substance of the gospel proclaimed.

Vision Insight 043: Vision is much more than a marketing statement or motto, yet these tools can be important in communicating vision.

It is important to cast vision in a manner that connects with the audience of each congregation. As a vision statement is molded in response to visionary discernment and insight, it must be the breath of God that edits the words and phrases, and not a Madison Avenue marketing mindset.

The counterpoint, as stated above, is that vision must connect with people who may not have the same depth of God talk in their lifestyle as the deeply committed disciples who form the people of passion in congregations. Vision must be stated in words and stories that effectively communicate with those to whom God is sending you.

Key Points for Your Congregation

First, vision is a full sensory experience. To say a vision statement is a vision is to marginalize the beauty, power, and spiritual character of vision. True vision is experienced, and then only when you're ready for a tool to communicate it to the masses is it written.

Second, vision—when written—is best told through a story that illustrates the impact of the vision. In fact, each hearer needs to be encouraged to develop his or her own story about vision.

Third, it is not the quality of a professionally written statement that will pull a congregation forward to its full Kingdom potential. It is people who are captured by the story of vision with their full heart, soul, mind, and strength.

Call to Action for Your Congregation

How would you state the vision of your congregation in your own words that is consistent with the way others would state the vision? What images, metaphors, stories, and life experiences best express for you the vision of your congregation? Take some time occasionally to think through your future story of ministry. If it helps, journal your thoughts and even a story or statement that works for you. Particularly think about how a person you know would be impacted by the vision of your congregation.

A Prayer for Your Congregation

Ever-present God, I want to be more like the Son. I not only want to believe in Jesus, I want to be a passionate follower of Jesus. Help me sense the type of vision You molded in Him about his messiahship. May the vision I experience within my congregation be one that honors, models, and embraces the spirit of the life and ministry of Jesus. May I accept the nudging of the Holy Spirit for our congregational vision to be challenging, transformational, and impactful for Your Kingdom. With thanksgiving for You, our Triune God, I pray. Amen.

CHAPTER FIVE

Excellent Versus Mediocre Visions

Vision is not about "good enough is good enough"

Timothy Lee, his wife Melinda, their three children, plus three families from their congregation intentionally moved together more than 2,500 miles from their homes to a place they felt God was calling them to start a new congregation.

It was in a fast-growing edge city in a metropolitan area of more than one million population. The vision by which they were captured involved starting a congregation with a contemporary style, small groups meeting in homes, missional engagement in their community context, and focused on people under 35 years old.

Eleven years later when I first met Timothy, 2,500 were attending their church and they were totally out of worship, education, fellowship and parking space. Their networking in the new city had connected them with a wealthy Christian entrepreneur who wanted to start a Christian school connected with a church. The merger of these two ideas was immediately successful.

Timothy's challenge was that he had never been pastor of a congregation of more than 500 in average attendance. He had no idea what to do next, or how to lead something this big. Yet, he knew God was still up to something and he needed to understand the next season of the congregation's life. He wanted it to be excellent and not mediocre. He wanted it to be where God was leading them and not where he personally wanted the congregation to go.

Today their weekly worship services have more than 10,000 people present in three locations in a 20-mile radius. Humongous numbers were not Timothy's goal. People just kept coming despite his own limitations, and those of his staff and lay leadership. Being pastor of a congregation captured by God's vision was his goal. Having an excellent versus mediocre vision was his desire.

What Are Excellent Versus Mediocre Congregational Visions?

I do not follow horse racing, or bet on horses. I leave that to people with money to burn, who probably also buy lottery tickets. Except . . .

Three Saturday afternoons per year I am positioned in front of a television to watch the running of the Triple Crown. I got infected with this virus by living in Louisville, KY for six years and catching Kentucky Derby fever. Watching champion thoroughbred horses run—particularly when they play a race back in slow motion—is watching artistic beauty.

It also happens that I lived in Louisville in 1973 when Secretariat won the Triple Crown. That year and every year since unless prohibited by my schedule, I watch the Kentucky Derby, the Preakness Stakes, and the Belmont Stakes.

Secretariat represented excellence rather than mediocrity. The Kentucky Derby is 1 1/4th miles, the Preakness Stakes is 1 3/16th miles, but the Belmont Stakes is 1 1/2 miles. Usually horses get a four-week rest after a significant race. The Triple Crown races are all held within five weeks of one another.

Experts felt in 1973 that Secretariat could not win the Belmont Stakes and thus the Triple Crown because of that rigorous race schedule, and the length of that third race. It turns out the opposite was true. Secretariat not only won the race, but did so by 31 lengths running away from the field.

Secretariat was not about business as usual. He not only won the Triple Crown, but did so with record times. Secretariat and excellent vision are both in exceptional categories.

George W. Bullard Jr.

Vision is not about business as usual. It is not about average thinking. It does not involve doing a little better next year than you did last year. It is not about mediocrity. It is not about pushing forward.

Vision is about excellence in response to God's empowering visionary leadership. It is about meeting the real needs of real people in real time. It is about doing the very best your capacities will empower within you. It is about increasing your capacities to strengthen your effectiveness in service. It is about expanding your capacities and deepening the excellence of your vision fulfillment.

Excellence is not only about outputs. It is about having a positive and challenging impact on the ability of congregations to serve in the midst of God's Kingdom. It is about building leadership capacities to increase and deepen the areas of ministry service. It is about developing sustainability patterns so that what you are doing is not just a short-term fix, but a long-term solution.

Here are five *Vision Insights* that focus on excellent congregational visions versus mediocre statements.

Vision Insight 044: When vision is of an excellent, challenging future, then you are more likely to get an excellent, challenging future.

Mediocrity should never be the character and nature of vision. Mediocrity is never the character and nature of the call of God upon a congregation.

An easily reached, unchallenging horizon should never be the limit of vision's sight. Vision always challenges congregations beyond that which they can see as they view the horizon before them.

The excellent, challenging character and nature of vision is a self-fulfilling prophecy. If you believe deeply in God's empowering vision and are committed to an excellent, challenging future then you are more likely to experience one. If you are only looking for a future that is good enough, then that is what you will accept.

Vision Insight 045: When vision is of an excellent, challenging future, then a more vital and vibrant future is a strong possibility.

If spiritual vitality and missional vibrancy are among the most desired characteristics of congregations then a vision of an excellent, challenging future is essential. Vitality and vibrancy do not happen by accident or through magical acts. They are largely the result of intentional effort in response to God's leading.

A vision of vitality and vibrancy moves us beyond doing OK or simply being healthy to a *FaithSoaring* journey that may allow congregations to approach God's full Kingdom potential.

- **Words and Ideas:** What is meant by *"FaithSoaring"* and *"FaithSoaring Church?"*

Vision Insight 046: When vision is of an excellent, challenging future, then more quality, depth, and quantity is a strong possibility.

Excellent, challenging visions—when acted on with positive intentionality that aligns everything congregations do to fulfill or live into their God-given vision—often result in greater quality, depth, and even quantitative growth.

Mediocre visions that do not empower congregations fail to achieve quality, depth, and an increased quantity of people who want to connect with a Christ-centered movement.

Too often congregational visions are about doing the same things in the same ways with the same leaders targeting the same people. This is not excellence. Congregational visions must involve doing new things in new ways with new leaders targeting new people.

Vision Insight 047: When vision is of an excellent, challenging future, then the congregation is continually seeking God's presence and leadership.

One way to determine the rightness and goodness of congregational vision is when it becomes obvious a congregation is seeking God's presence and leadership as the primary focus of their congregation. Excellent visions are about God's spiritual strategic direction, and not the direction of humankind.

One way to ascertain that congregations do not have a vision of an excellent, challenging future is that they appear to accommodate the desires of strong personalities within their midst rather than focus on the obvious leadership of God. The vision of some congregations is co-opted by loud, strong, controlling voices.

Vision Insight 048: When vision is of an excellent, challenging future, then it can positively impact the spirituality of the congregation.

Congregations with an excellent, challenging vision from God do not become more secular in their perspectives and patterns. They become more spiritual. They understand they are not a business. They are a spiritual community with the exceptional DNA of having become captured by God's empowering vision.

They generally also experience an ever-deeper spirituality. This sets them apart from other organizations in a wonderful way. Part of their mission and vision is to make God's entire world more loving and just. They care obviously and deeply about people everywhere.

When It Comes to Congregational Vision, Good Enough is Never Good Enough

Surely you have heard the expression throughout your life that something is "good enough for government work."

This phrase has come to represent mediocrity so strongly that no one would believe you if you told them that at one time it referred instead to rigorous standards that had to be met. But it did.

When people think about congregational vision do they think about mediocrity or excellence? Because becoming captured by God's empowering vision is difficult, too often people work on it for a while and then say something like "that is good enough for church work." That defines congregational vision as sufficiently unimportant that it is fine to be mediocre. For God the opposite is true.

Vision Insight 049: When it comes to vision, good enough is never good enough, adequate is never acceptable, and mediocrity is never excellence.

In chapter three I referred to my work at the national missions agency of my denomination. Excellence was our standard as we worked to fulfill the mission and vision embodied in the Great Commission.

When I moved to a state level missional role I was shocked to discover the measuring rod was extremely different. What we considered mediocre at the national agency was excellence in the state.

That gap in the understanding of excellence made it very difficult to engage in leading edge missional efforts. When I led my team to excellence we were criticized by others who did not appreciate the competition and the higher benchmark we were setting. As one colleague who led another team said to me, "When you get too far out in front of us, you make a good target. We have guns and an itchy trigger finger."

Vision Insight 050: When vision is of a mediocre, business-as-usual future, you will get a mediocre, business-as-usual future.

When I pushed for excellence in this regional denominational role I got push back from many places, even from within my own team. I was most disappointed with staff who did not want to work hard enough and smart enough to achieve true excellence. My staff team was criticized for our hard work and for demanding excellence.

The criticism was so strong that—with the permission of the CEO—some of our work went underground so we could continue achieving excellence

George W. Bullard Jr.

and making Kingdom progress without making ourselves a target for delays by other staff.

Vision Insight 051: When vision is of a mediocre, business-as-usual future, then you get a future less vital and vibrant than you projected.

One of the signs of mediocrity in my denominational organization was in the area that sponsored the special missions offering among the churches that funded about half of our missional efforts. The year before I arrived their offering raised about $777,000. Their goal, however, for the next year was only $700,000.

I questioned this. It did not appear challenging. The director's response was that they set their goals low to be sure they were met. I realized I had just witnessed mediocrity personified.

Their work and ministry had been plateaued and declining for several years at that point. They wondered why. I could have told them. In fact, mediocrity might have been a step up for them. Fortunately, a new director with a high commitment to excellence was soon elected to replace the retiring director.

Vision Insight 052: When vision is of a mediocre, business-as-usual future, then less is less and more is nowhere in sight.

I was shocked one day when a colleague wanted to hold up as excellent a congregation that was so mediocre it might have to close within a year or two. I visited the congregation and discovered their goal was a mediocre, business-as-usual future. They saw nothing beyond mediocrity.

Too many people want to be liked so much they affirm and bless mediocrity to gain or retain good relationships. I believe while God desires for us to proactively love one another unconditionally, that we also hold one another accountable to achieve leading edge prophetic service.

Vision Insight 053: When vision is of a mediocre, business-as-usual future, the congregation may be turning its back on the call of God.

What do too many congregations do when God calls them to a prophetic, innovative vision for Kingdom progress? They lie down beside it and go to sleep. They declare they cannot do what God wants them to do. They declare this is their church and they will do what they want to do, not realizing such an attitude makes them insubordinate regarding God's leadership.

Yes, it is important for congregations to realize they cannot do everything, that God is also calling forward others. Yet whatever vision it is that we are called to fulfill deserves our most excellent effort, and with the obvious implication we are captured by it.

Vision Insight 054: When vision is of a mediocre, business-as-usual future, it can negatively impact the spirituality of the congregation.

If the vision of a congregation is mediocre, characterized by business as usual, then expectation of spiritual maturity among members is likely low. Cutting edge innovation in the spiritual formation, leadership development, and missional engagement of congregations is not required amidst low expectations.

If vision is of an excellent future, characterized by an exceptional congregational journey, then expectations of spiritual maturity among congregational participants will be high. Leading edge innovation in spiritual formation, leadership development, and missional engagement is most likely present in high expectation congregations.

Key Points for Your Congregation

First, with congregational life now holding only the fourth or fifth priority in the lives of many people, finding enough spiritual passion for congregations to have excellent rather than mediocre visions can be a challenge. Only excellent visions will suffice and honor our Triune God.

Second, the mediocre vision accepted by many congregations is a self-fulfilling prophecy. If the vision is mediocre, then a mediocre congregation will result. If the vision is excellent, then the possibility exists for an excellent congregation.

Third, the saddest part of a mediocre vision is that it may result in a congregation full of mediocre Christians who are more nominally Christian than they are mature followers of Jesus. Some congregations aim low and others aim high. The difference is often dramatic.

Call to Action for Your Congregation

At times vision needs to be developed in rounds. In round one seek to discern what God is calling your congregation to be and do. Once you think you have it, set that vision aside, and start dreaming about unseen things that could take your congregation way past the initial vision discernment.

Be careful you are not talking first about numbers. Numbers are a consequence of your spiritual and strategic journey and not the focus of the journey. Perhaps by round three you will begin to sense God's empowering vision.

A Prayer for Your Congregation

Oh God, you are no small God. You are unmeasurable in Your love and greatness. We want a vision that honors You, and calls upon all our spiritual gifts to create a transformational congregation. What is that for us? What is Your will for our Christ-centered fellowship? What defines excellence for us in our context? Reveal Your vision to us in such a way that we will understand the majesty of our service to You in response to that vision. We strive for the excellence only You can provide. Amen.

CHAPTER SIX

Vision is Not About Programs
and Management

Congregations cannot push their way into God's future

I once was invited to a meeting in a congregation I was consulting and asked to be ready to answer questions about the strategic planning process in which the church was engaged.

When everyone got into the room, the people present were myself, the executive pastor, the senior pastor, the chair of the church council, the chair of the finance committee, the chair of the trustees, and two persons I had not yet met. It turns out one was the immediate past chair of the finance committee.

The other was a mystery man. I eventually learned this man once held each of the lay leadership positions now held by the others in this meeting. He now had no position, but was the king-maker. Everyone present and serving in their roles had been recruited or approved by him.

Currently he came to worship less than once per month. He owned a house at the beach and another in the mountains. That is where he and his wife liked to be on weekends. Whether or not he was in attendance, he oversaw what programs got funding and what decisions were made.

This was an informal executive committee, and he was the chairperson. They had absolute authority which they had wrestled away from the official structure of the church. During the meeting, they gave orders to both the senior pastor and the executive pastor as to what they were to do about certain matters.

I came to discover that very few people even knew this group existed. Yet, they influenced everything that happened in the church, and never lost a battle over any issue. They ran church programs and management like it was a closely held corporation and they were the self-perpetuating board of directors.

At the same time, they were clueless about the spiritual side of the congregation. They felt discipleship was an activity for those too weak to make hard decisions. When it came to vision, they wondered what God had to do with it. They knew where the congregation needed to go, and they were taking it there as the dominant "first church" of their denomination in their town.

They represent the antithesis of everything you are reading in this book. Their name is Legion as many congregations harbor such an individual or group. They see the congregation as an organization to manage, and not a spiritual organism responding to God's leadership. They are all about programs and management.

Congregational Vision is About Expanding and Deepening Disciplemaking

Vision is not about promoting programs and using an attractional approach to engage in a spiritual and strategic journey. It is not about a focus on operational planning, or focusing on systems management.

Vision is about expanding and deepening the relationships of the congregation with God and one another in your context. It is about the people who are impacted through a disciplemaking process rather than getting more people to attend discipleship events. It is not about programmatic success, but disciplemaking significance.

Recently a congregation considered a choice to promote an attractional approach for growing their congregation, or a missional approach to connect both with people needing ministry and people interested in their ministry. They chose the attractional approach. The perceived challenge was about what they could do to make their church successful, rather than how they could make it more significant in the lives of the people.

The attractional approach is about generating programmatic success. The missional approach is about generating disciplemaking significance. Which would you choose? Why?

Vision is not about doing things right. That is the mantra of management. Vision is about doing the right things that help people grow in the grace and knowledge of Jesus Christ in the spirit of 2 Peter 3:18.

Vision Insight 055: Having a proactive, excellent call to disciplemaking action plus experiences that live into vision is as important as casting vision.

A vast difference exists between a vision that is stated and a vision that becomes real and alive through a call to action.

I had a very interesting dialogue with a pastor I was coaching about the difference between a vision stated and a vision realized. His congregation was struggling because of the success of a new contemporary worship service. They did many things right along the way. They had three worship services, each a different style with a different target group.

A challenge arose when the contemporary worship service outgrew its space and needed to swap places with the gospel service that focused on senior adults. While having distinct worship services meeting in various locations in the facilities had been a fine idea, when the contemporary worship service became the largest of the three and attendees made the highest per capita financial contributions to the church, that was more than long-tenured, older members could stand.

Conflict arose. The pastor prayerfully struggled with what to do. He came up with a vision of one unified worship service to replace the three. The sanctuary could hold everyone. He was anxious about sharing it with his congregation. In our ongoing dialogue, I realized I needed to ask him, "Do you have to have this vision, or do you have to faithfully state it because you feel God has given it to you?"

He said he had to faithfully state it. Which he did. That was not what the congregation ended up doing. But it led to a solution.

Vision Insight 056: Vision is more about increasing and deepening disciplemaking than it is about successful and growing programs.

Program fulfillment is an inadequate call to action. Programs are seldom if ever the pathway to fulfilling vision. Not in our world. Fulfilling vision is about discipleship development involving spiritual formation, leadership development, and missional engagement.

Vision fulfillment should lead with a focus on developing adult disciples and empowering discipleship in other age groups. Congregations need excellent programs, ministries, and activities for everyone from birth to death. Yet the goal of programs should not be their own success and growth.

The goal should be to deepen the spiritual formation, leadership development, and missional engagement of followers of Jesus Christ. Effective programs, ministries, and activities that meet the real needs of real people in real time are the methods and not the result.

Vision Insight 057: Many congregations fall back on their mission statement as their vision, rather than being embraced by a specific vision that includes disciplemaking.

Mission statements, which should express a generic overarching sense of the mission of God for congregations, can easily fail to move beyond nice words and feelings to become a specific call to action for prophetic contextual service. Mission statements are too general without a clear vision plus strategies and tactics that fulfill the vision. A clear call to action is essential.

One church had a mission statement and considered that enough. Their self-evaluation of their mission went something like this: "While we do not have a clear measurement of progress in fulfillment of our mission, with all the faithful actions and some successful programs we have experienced, surely we have moved forward as a congregation." Evaluative comments like this can be made right up until the day the church closes and locks it doors for the last time.

Congregational Vision is Not About Successfully Growing Programs

Many congregations believe the best way to make progress is to have excellent programs, ministries, and activities. They measure the success of their congregation by the quantitative and qualitative strength of their programs.

They work hard. They push the congregation forward. They focus on an attractional approach. If they do not use the term church growth, they use another term like being "inviting" as the focus of what they do.

They believe if they could only have high quality preschool, children, and youth programs they will bring the success of God's Kingdom into their congregation. They press for short-term gains. They build or renovate buildings every time the tactical approach to programs changes.

They can do all of this, but if they have no vision they may not be going anywhere. Yet, both staff and laity are often codependent for their own focus and daily work structure on the programs, ministries, and activities they have institutionalized into the culture of their congregation. They do not know how to do it another way. They panic when they think about not having the programs they have counted on for so many years.

Regardless of the new things God is doing in their midst, regardless of the reality that their programs are not working anymore and not connecting with people, they still want to do the same programs. They cannot visualize their congregation without them. Staff is afraid they cannot justify their job without a lot of programs.

Vision Insight 058: Vision is more about relationships with God, one another, and your context than it is about successful programs.

If the journey of a congregation is a sports utility vehicle—a metaphor I use regularly—then "vision" is driving and fueling the forward progress of the vehicle. "Relationships" is in the navigation seat next to the driver flavoring the style of the journey and the relationship to God, and one another, and the community context.

"Programs" are intended to be in support roles to relationships. They're in the back seat. Programs proactively empower the opportunity for meaningful relationships to occur. They are not the goal or the navigator. They are supportive. If they ever become the goal or navigator it is because the congregation is visionless. "Management" is also in the back seat behind vision. We will address this role later.

Vision Insight 059: Many congregations structure their life around programs rather than relationships, thus putting a drag factor on vision.

Too many programs drag down congregations. They create busy-ness that can be exhausting. They create a need for single use space that shackles the congregation under debt or mammoth fundraising efforts. They burn out both staff and lay volunteers.

Not long ago I sat in a congregational staff meeting where a relatively new staff person described the pressure he felt during his first year and the physical illnesses he experienced trying to keep up with all the programs and make them successful.

One process I use with many congregations is *100 Days of Discernment using Dialogue and Prayer Triplets*. This involves as many members as possible participating in dialogue and prayer triplets which meet 10 times over 100 days for at least an hour guided by various issues about the future of the congregation.

- **Words and Ideas:** See more about the *100 Days of Discernment Using Dialogue and Prayer Triplets*.

One of the inevitable outcomes in almost every congregation is the declaration that the congregation needs to decrease the number of programs to allow for a more open informal process of dialogue and prayer.

Vision Insight 060: Programs, processes, and emphases in a congregation must have their own vision that supports the congregation's vision.

One of the key aspects of vision fulfillment or living into God's empowering vision is that everything the congregation does must align with the vision. This is so much better than marching off in separate directions.

That means, as an example, the music ministry must support the congregational vision. The youth ministry must support the congregational vision. The missional engagements must support the congregational vision. I could go on.

The human resources team of one congregation, once it had been captured by vision, asked each staff person to prioritize his or her written position description. They were to indicate the new things they needed to start doing to fulfill the vision, the things they needed to stop doing, and how they could rethink existing things to help them better support God's empowering vision for the congregation.

Vision Insight 061: It is easy to confuse having vision with the success of programs, ministries, and activities. They are not the same.

Many congregations I encounter believe they are captured by vision because they can point to multiple successful programs, ministries, and activities. When I share the sports utility vehicle metaphor with them they vow and declare programs are driving the vehicle that is their congregation. What better vision, they say, can we have than these successful programs?

Be not confused. Successful programs do not a vision make. Vision transcends programs, ministries, and activities. Completed checklists, specific tactics, personal style is not the essence of vision. They are just details you may need to support vision fulfillment.

Congregations Cannot Manage Their Way into God's Future for Them

Where there is no vision in the driver's seat, management slides behind the wheel and vision now occupies management's spot in the back seat. When this happens, many managers are elated. They believe they should have been in the driver's seat all along to keep programs humming and budgets in line.

For a while relationships are still navigating from the right-front seat, but eventually programs will move into the navigation seat. Relationships will be overtaken by tasks. Process will be overturned by programs.

The difficulty is that no congregation can manage its way into the future God has for them. This is pushing when God is about pulling. Management is about efficiency whereas vision is about excellence. Management is about an organizational focus, and vision is about an organism or movement focus.

Management in the lead is simply the opposite of having vision in the lead. While important, management processes are not intended to lead. They are intended to support visionary leadership.

My observation over the decades is that few management people in congregations are also involved in an ongoing process of deepening their personal discipleship. Their organizational management experience has not helped them understand the ministry passion and involvement of congregational staff. It does not fit their task-oriented organizational pattern. They do not believe the congregational staff works enough.

Here are three *Vision Insights* that suggest a focus on management in congregations is not a focus on God's empowering vision.

Vision Insight 062: Management is only fully happy when it is driving the congregational vehicle. When not driving, it is trying to drive.

Management has an overwhelming desire to be in charge. Management believes congregations need more of what it can offer. Management feels leaders are not accountable, and are not leading.

Even if a congregation is being well led, management people still feel leaders are not paying attention to all the right things. They continue to urge greater efficiencies, and they are partially right. But they are not sufficiently right that their concerns should always be addressed as a priority.

In the patterns of congregational life developed over generations, there are times when management must lead because there is no vision, or there are insufficient leaders to empower the vision. When this happens the driving actions of management are meant to be temporary to provide a respite for visionary leaders to renew their strength and soar with faith like eagles. (See Isaiah 40:28-31.)

But management does not want to give up the driver's seat to a new, emerging sense of God's empowering vision for the congregation. So, they may oppose the emerging vision, saying it is risky and out of character for the congregation.

Vision Insight 063: Vision fulfillment is about empowerment over control, relationships over programs, and hope over heritage.

Empowerment, relationships, and hope are the currency of vision. Control, complicated administration and decision-making, over programming, and too high a view of the congregation's heritage is the currency of management. Congregations are often over managed by controlling leaders, and under led by fuzzy visionary leadership.

Too often a management approach seeks to move a congregation merely from negative to neutral. Management is concerned about fixing what is wrong rather than discovering and soaring with what is right and good.

The classic—and overused—statement true of management in many congregations is, "We've never done it that way before." The heritage culture has infected many congregations. God's empowering vision is about hope that builds on the heritage rather than the hope that heritage will one day return the congregation to dominance.

Vision Insight 064: Effective visionary leadership is supported by empowering management that is captured by God's empowering vision for the congregation.

Management can be empowering and not controlling. For many congregations that is an unfamiliar concept. They primarily experience management as controlling.

It is a thing of great beauty when management people, administrative committees, or governance groups are captured by the vision of the congregation, and see the great contribution they can make to empowering fulfillment of that vision.

Unfortunately, management leaders in too many congregations see it as their responsibility to control rather than empower the congregation. In its most radical form this control can be demonic. Where management people may be partially right is when visionary leadership engages in sloppy management practices.

God's empowering vision seeks to empower congregations to be all they can be in the midst of God's Kingdom. Satan seeks to control congregations and keep them from doing well and being people of Good News.

Congregational Management Must Be Accountable to Visionary Leadership

"Who is in charge here?" shouts the man in TV dramas who comes into a situation where he obviously wants to be in charge.

Early in the US presidency of Ronald Reagan we came to know this as the *Alexander Haig Syndrome*. Haig was Reagan's Secretary of State. When the assassination attempt was made on Reagan on March 30, 1981, Haig was asked by White House reporters "Who is in charge?" while the president was incapacitated in the hospital. He famously declared, "I'm in charge." Of course, this was constitutionally incorrect, and the country never let Haig forget it.

Within organizations there is a frequent call for greater accountability and supervision. People must be called upon to follow the plan, do their part, do it right, and do it now. At its worst this is a form of management that trusts leadership only if they are the leaders. They want to reimage congregational leadership into their own image.

Too many times I have heard stories of laypersons with a demand and command mindset who try to tell the pastor and staff how they must do their job. They may even throw in a little "or else" talk.

One type of these people is those who sometime during their 50s discovered they were never going to achieve the career goal they thought they deserved and they became angry. They could not make their boss recognize their genius, and someone less deserving was promoted over them.

Over the years they could not make anyone on the job follow their demands but they sure could make their congregation stand up and listen. They had power there. The congregation must listen.

Congregations are where the visionary leadership initiated by God and championed by leaders needs to be respected and followed. Here are three *Vision Insights* that suggest a focus on management's accountability to visionary leadership in congregations.

Vision Insight 065: Vision is about leadership rather than management. Management should be accountable to visionary leadership.

Visionary leadership should take the initiative. Management is accountable to visionary leadership rather than visionary leadership being accountable to management.

Too few management people see it this way, which is why so many congregations have what would be called a low ceiling. They want a controllable environment and not a lot of changes. Yet, when the Holy Spirit is inspiring leaders, and they understand their initiating role in helping the congregation see vision, they need a place where there is no ceiling and innovation is unlimited in the long-term.

Vision Insight 066: When visionary leadership is not present in a congregation, it creates a vacuum into which management rushes.

Management is the heaviest weight class in congregations, and knows how to throw a punch. It knows how to takeover. When management is given an opening, it rushes into the vacuum created by the lack of vision.

At times the ability of management to take over is a good thing. If leadership is weak and directionless, congregations may need management to rush in and do something. Almost anything. But it should be temporary until vision can mount up with wings as eagles, and soar with faith, as referenced earlier.

Vision Insight 067: Living into vision is not about a checklist of tasks, but a map for a scavenger hunt that moves from experience to experience.

Don't turn vision into a left-brained operational plan focused on tasks. Vision is more a right-brained adventure that feels the presence and leadership of God. It is a journey. It follows its God-given values.

It tells stories. It has meaningful interaction within the fellowship of the congregation, in its community context, or among the demographic groups with whom it ministers. It seeks to do its part to make the world more loving and just.

Many models of long-range and strategic planning have action or operational plans that involve a checklist of actions to be completed. They are about output. They are about management.

Vision is about impact. When a portion of the plan or story is completed then evaluate. Recast the vision and the strategy that supports it. Move forward beyond the initial horizon to new horizons that now can be visualized. This is leadership.

Neither Bigger Barns nor Towers of Babel Produce Congregational Vision

Congregational vision is not about bigger barns. The rich man with an abundance of crops, found in the parable in Luke 12:16-21, was proud of his harvest and wanted to retain much more of it. So, he built bigger barns.

The parable tells us the man was about storing more treasure for himself rather than being rich regarding his soul relationship with God. Vision is not about bigger buildings, larger endowments, more staff, or even a radically growing membership. It is about being rich in God's sight rather than the sight of humankind. God's richness for us focuses our vision.

Or, take the story of the Tower of Babel in Genesis 11:1-9. Humankind wanted to build a tower that would reach into the heavens. They wanted to make a name for themselves rather than to glorify God's name. Ultimately it led to confusion rather than clarity, to people's inability to understand one another, to greater diversity and diffusion throughout the world, and to a lack of unity.

The desire to build bigger barns and taller towers was not fulfilling. Only later do we hear a clear call to store up for ourselves treasure in heaven with the declaration that where our treasure is will be where our heart is also. (See Matthew 6:19-21.)

Bigger barns and taller towers are a biblical example of the movie the *Field of Dreams*, from which comes the statement, "If you build it, they will come." Many congregations construct new buildings with the same feeling that it we build it they will come. The "they" are new guests who become members who produce numerical growth and financial success for the congregation.

Do not misunderstand. Nothing is wrong with having high quality spacious buildings if that is what congregational ministry in your context among a specific group of people requires for effective ministry. It is just that buildings should neither be the focus of our vision nor the measurement of the success of our vision. Buildings can be absent or destroyed and our vision can still be strong, fulfilling, and significant.

Here are two *Vision Insights* that suggest a focus on buildings in congregations is not a focus on God's empowering vision.

Vision Insight 068: Vision is not about new or retrofitted buildings, but about the lives transformed through the ministries that take place within these buildings.

Management likes to see new tangible things happening. New or retrofitted buildings is visible evidence of growth and progress. Buildings may be to some people an obvious sign of progress, but they represent another way to walk by sight rather than to walk by faith. (See 2 Corinthians 5:7.) As such they can be a hindrance to vision fulfillment.

Vision is about transformed lives. Such transformation is not as easy to see as new buildings. It is easy for people to miss the new, spiritual, and innovative things happening in hearts and congregations. Too often we are looking at the outward appearance rather than the inward heart.

Vision Insight 069: A vision for a needed or wanted new or retrofitted building is seldom, if ever, a missional vision that is pulling the congregation forward. Buildings are tools that flow out of vision.

Buildings are not usually missional. There may be a few exceptions—just not as many exceptions as people who like new or retrofitted buildings think there are.

Many church leaders—both clergy and laity—believe one of the easiest ways to motivate congregations is to put a building project before them. Challenge people to raise money. Urge people to pray for the building project. I encounter pastors who think every church ought always to have debt because servicing debt kept tithes and offerings higher.

Once I was visiting a church with a potential consultant to raise funds for a new education and fellowship building. It was needed. The current building had been in such disrepair for many years that it needed to be torn down and replaced. The space was essential for both current and potential programs.

Much of the dialogue was about square footage, technology, and décor. It was obvious the people at the gathering were not getting a vision for the building. Those trying to sell it to them were selling a facility and not a vision.

The pastor's first grandchild was at the meeting in the arms of her mother. Since the new building space was to be primarily for education and fellowship programs. I suggested we visualize the pastor's grandchild as a maturing Christian growing partially through the spiritual formation that could happen in this new building. Participants got it and began to talk about other people who would be impacted, and what form that impact might take.

The building is not the vision. Transformed lives is the vision.

Key Points for Your Congregation

First, the idea of programs as an effective way for congregations to be vital and vibrant started dying in the 1960s. By the 1970s they had lost their role as the primary way for congregations to be faithful, effective, and innovative. Still yet, many congregations believe vision is about successful programs and management, when it is about disciplemaking.

Second, programs in congregations can be numerically successful, even while the congregation is missing being significant in God's Kingdom, and totally missing the concept of full surrender to God in their life and ministry.

Third, management in congregations—as it is in many other organizations—is about efficiency. Vision supported by spiritual formation, leadership development, and missional engagement is about effectiveness.

Call to Action for Your Congregation

Engage your congregation in a total program and management reset. Start with a blank sheet of paper that has no programs or management structure on it. Dialogue about what programs and management structures are essential to fulfilling your God-given vision, and helping every possible person to develop as a Christian disciple. Any program or management structure that does not contribute to vision and disciplemaking should not exist.

A Prayer for Your Congregation

Lord Jesus, Son of God, I cannot remember any place in the Gospels where you established programs. I do not read about a management structure except for someone to be treasurer. The treasurer role obviously did not work out well in the case of Judas. What you did was to help people grow in grace and knowledge. Help us to be that kind of congregation as we seek to live into God's empowering vision. Amen.

CHAPTER SEVEN

Living into God's Empowering Vision

Celebrate vision fulfillment without ceasing

Too many congregations have their vision and intentionality out of whack. Even when they seem to be captured by God's empowering vision, they fail to understand that means they must do things differently than they did before. Being captured by vision is not enough. Congregations also must intentionally live into that vision.

Providence was a congregation I would place in the category of a 50-plus congregation. These are congregations where 80 percent or more of the attendees are 50 years old or more. Motivated to seek a new vision for the future they had successfully developed an understanding of God's empowering vision for them. However, it did not seem to be making any difference in their vitality and vibrancy.

During a coaching conference call I asked them to list the top priority programs, ministries, and activities in which they were engaging to live into that vision. After a few minutes, I stopped the conversation, and said I wanted to know about the things they were doing that fulfilled their vison.

To my dismay, they said the items they just listed *were* fulfilling their mission. I then asked them to tell me the new things they were doing based on their understanding of God's empowering vision. They said they were not doing anything new. They were just doing the old things with more excitement because they had vision. It was clearly another example of insanity where someone does the same things repeatedly and expects different results.

A more recent congregation I worked with—Christ the King—gave me more hope. They said early in their process they wanted to re-evaluate all their programs, ministries, and activities prior to developing their future story of ministry. Then they would eliminate the ones that do not fit the vision, focus on those that do, and add only those things that would help them live into God's empowering vision for them.

Congregational Vision is About the Journey Towards Fulfillment

The goal of congregational vision is not only to be captured by God's empowering vision but to live into that vision humbly and proudly. It is about doing what the vision inspires in congregations. It is about the fulfillment of a spiritual and strategic journey.

Being captured by God's empowering vision is insufficient. Vision is the beginning of the journey and not the end. Living into the vision is your journey towards fulfillment.

Many congregations have some semblance of a vision, and then they invest their energy and resources in something different. Living into your congregational vision means you align your processes, programs, ministries, and activities to fulfill your vision.

In congregations seeking to fulfill their vision, leaders are recruited for the journey to fulfillment with the key criteria that they are captured by the vision, and they minister in a manner that will fulfill the vision. They are committed to aligning all their leadership activities with the vision.

Here are four *Vision Insights* that illustrate various aspects of living into a vision and seeking to journey towards fulfillment.

Vision Insight 070: Leaders sold out to their congregation's vision often think about how they can help fulfill God's empowering vision.

A high percentage of leaders in a congregation should be sold out to the fulfillment of the vision. It cannot be a few. It must be at least 21 percent of the average number of adults present on a typical weekend for worship. In smaller membership congregations with less than 100 adults in attendance, it needs to be at least 21 adults. Leaders sold out to the vision have positive spiritual passion towards the vision. The hope is that this 21 percent number will grow as the envisioning process progresses.

Vision Insight 071: Vision and its fulfillment should positively impact every decision a congregation makes or vision becomes marginalized.

When it comes to congregational wide decisions, it is a winning combination if both leaders and non-leaders are asking how their decisions will help fulfill the vision. While using this measuring approach for the rightness and goodness of a vision can be taken too far, few congregations are in danger of doing so. More congregations need to be taking the risk of asking about decisions and actions, and how they relate to vision fulfillment.

It is certainly a lot better than people asking how decisions and actions will result in no change and no impact on them. Or, asking how decisions and actions bring back yesterday.

Vision Insight 072: A congregation captured by vision is always asking in every dimension of ministry how decisions and actions will help them fulfill their vision.

Beyond congregational wide decisions, every time a team, program, or governance group makes a decision they should always ask the question, "How will this decision and the action it calls for help us live into our overall congregational vision and journey towards its fulfillment?"

If a decision or action does not empower the congregational vision and its fulfillment, it should be questioned, reconsidered, and perhaps not done. While not everything a congregation does must fulfill the vision, everything it does must stand the test of how it could possibly empower the vision.

Vision Insight 073: Vision should be the main framework and focus of a congregation's actions and not just part of the puzzle.

Vision is not that last piece to complete a 1,000-piece puzzle. It is not the piece that fell on the floor and was kicked under the sofa. It is the cornerstone piece placed first, and around which the framing is built and the puzzle is completed.

Vision is the cornerstone for bringing together the amazing puzzle of a congregation composed of people with varying gifts, skills, and preferences. It's not just one of the things you are possessed by, but the essential characteristic of a congregation living with excitement into the journey God inspired in it.

Congregational Vision Fulfillment Should Be Celebrated Regularly and Often

Do you remember the place and time of a significant spiritual experience in your life? I remember some of them in my life, but not all. Some of my most significant spiritual experiences occurred in Gregory Memorial Baptist Church in Baltimore, MD where my father was pastor.

Our family spent 8.5 years in that church before moving on to Philadelphia. Many of my experiences were enhanced when we moved to Philadelphia when I was 15 years old, and I helped my parents start new churches. I have always felt I grew more spiritually in the last two years of high school while helping launch new congregations than most any other two-year period in my life.

If any period rivals the Philadelphia years, it was the 4.5 years I spent on the staff and then as pastor of an inner-city congregation in Louisville, KY while attending seminary. The cultural experiences bombarded my emotions, challenged my faith, and re-formed my theology. My adult ministry was framed by that ministry experience.

These experiences were 40 to 50 years ago. I cannot—and have not—relied on those experiences as the fulfillment of my spiritual walk with God.

They were foundational and formative. But they weren't the completion of my life journey. They were beginning steps.

I rejoice in the Lord in the depth of my current understanding of God's living Word—Jesus the Christ—and how as a follower of Jesus I celebrate regularly and often the spiritual experiences that continually amaze me.

This is the same for vision. When a congregation is captured by vision, that doesn't end their journey. It launches it anew. It is foundational and formational. As congregations live into the vision, regular and frequent celebrations should be held highlighting the new things God is doing in and through them.

Vision Insight 074: Living into vision requires regular spiritual celebration of the fulfillment of the future story of ministry for the congregation.

Vision must be continually cast. Vision should also be celebrated in some public way at least every 120 days. These celebrations should be spiritual in nature and should involve telling the stories of people who have been impacted by the journey towards vision fulfillment. They must also be characterized by a fellowship gathering that celebrates the congregation as community.

Regular spiritual celebrations should include worship of the Triune God, and a spirit of thankfulness for what God is doing in and through the congregation. Remember that vision fulfillment is not an organizational journey of humankind. It is a spiritual journey by a living, breathing, moving, ever-changing Christ-centered and faith-based organism.

Vision Insight 075: Vision not used to evaluate the goodness and rightness of congregational decisions will not remain the vision for long.

Around the time of these every 120-day celebrations the journey of vision fulfillment should also be evaluated. As stories are shared, what is the evidence of the goodness and rightness of congregational decisions and actions? How is the congregation doing at aligning decisions and actions around the vision? Are any course corrections needed?

Regular evaluation of decisions and actions is essential, as well as adjusting the trajectory of the congregation's journey to keep it focused on vision fulfillment. Without doing so the vision can take a negative detour.

Vision Insight 076: During a visionary journey God at times changes our plans and heads us to a new Macedonia as told in Acts 16:9-10.

It is possible your understanding of the vision and its fulfillment can change. This can happen in at least two ways.

First, the congregation may have misunderstood the long-term implications of the vision. They may get off track from God's empowering vision, and must adjust the vision to stay focused on God's leadership.

Second, it is also possible within God's circumstantial will that changes in the situation of the congregation, the context of the congregation, and the spiritual maturity of the congregation may call for a new or refocused vision.

It is important that every seven years, or whenever there is a significant interruption in vision fulfillment, that congregations engage in a revisioning process to be sure they are on the right vision fulfillment journey, and to help newer people connected with the congregation own the vision more deeply.

Newcomers Who Connect with Congregations Need to Own the Vision

Many congregations have policies that require people to connect with their congregation for a certain amount of time before they are eligible to hold leadership positions. My church, for example, requires a person to be a member for at least one year before they qualify for core leadership positions.

These policies are both good news and bad. They are good because they ask people to get to know the church before they try to lead the church.

Also, they allow the church's current leaders to get to know them before placing them in a leadership position.

In some settings, such policies do not work well. For example, congregations in a highly transient area—such as around military bases—may not get these faithful and committed new members into leadership positions until right before they are transferred away. Tenure policies must be customized to the context.

One very important area where there should be no tenure requirement is in connecting newcomers with the congregational vision. The vision ought to be obvious to them from the first time they connect with the congregation. During their first worship service, or small group, or from information provided to them as a guest they should be presented with the vision and even have it interpreted for them.

Several reasons make this important. First, your existing members need to practice casting vision to new people. Since the focus is on a movement that is memorable rather than a statement that is memorized, vision can become fuzzy over time.

Second, it is the congregation's journey toward fulfilling the vision that provides the best example of the vision to share with newcomers. Third, newcomers must own the vision, too, particularly as they move into leadership roles, or soon the vision may no longer be sustainable. Congregations could get to a point that most active members are no longer captured by vision.

Vision Insight 077: Vision may always be a little fuzzy—particularly in the ways to fulfill it—because it is always looking beyond the current horizon.

A great, empowering vision talks about things yet unseen. When vision addresses things beyond the horizon that only God can see, it may be a little fuzzy to existing members.

Sometimes new people are quicker to see what lies beyond the horizon. They do not carry the congregation's cultural and historical baggage, which may give them better insight. It is why you always ask newcomers to describe what it was like to become connected with your congregation.

Vision Insight 078: Vision is continually clarified as a congregation journeys in the direction of God's future for them.

In the clarification of vision, often it is newcomers who can assist with that clarification. They can talk about how they experienced the vision fulfillment actions and affirm the actions that most attracted them to and assimilated them into the congregation.

While congregations think it is worship, preaching, Sunday School classes or small groups, often it is the sense of community and involvement in missional engagement that cement the relationship with newcomers. Relationships are so important!

Vision Insight 079: The sustainability of vision may be dependent on how well it is cast to and owned by newcomers in the congregation.

The ability of congregations to effectively cast their vision to newcomers may be the key factor in vision sustainability. Even with all the efforts and experiences to become captured by God's empowering vision for the congregation, if newcomers cannot embrace and internalize the vision it may be a short-term fix rather than a long-term solution.

For newcomers to internalize the vision they must quickly develop their own stories about how the vision is making a key difference in their spiritual lives. They must engage as participants and leaders in vision fulfillment actions. They must develop within their first six months to a year the ability to cast the vision in their own words.

They must be able to refer to the vision as "our" understanding of God's leadership, and not "their" understanding of God's leadership.

Congregational Vision Raises the Expectations of Disciples

Expectations of Christian disciples always go along with fulfillment of congregational vision. Few, if any, congregations who have low expectations of Christian disciples are likely to become captured by God's empowering vision for their future ministry, and to live prophetically into that vision.

Congregational vision calls for Christian disciples to engage, to be proactive, to be intentional, and to be faithful, effective, and innovative in fulfilling God's empowering vision for their congregation. Unfortunately, many disciples in churches are unengaged, passive, random, and lack faithfulness, effectiveness, and innovation.

Raising the expectations of Christian disciples is best if it comes because of God pulling them forward as opposed to church leaders pushing them forward. Disciples who are pushed do not usually give their full heart, soul, mind, and strength to the effort. That is why it is important to see the acquiring of and the living into vision as a spiritual process that matures and motivates disciples. It is easier to raise the expectations of Christian disciples if they were proactively involved in the vision casting and capturing process.

Here are three *Vision Insights* that speak to vision, expectations, and disciples.

Vision Insight 080: Living into vision involves an intentional disciplemaking process that seeks to help people grow spiritually.

I do not know of any vision from God that does not also invite, urge, and pull disciples forward to a more mature and spiritually deep lifestyle. Disciplemaking, becoming a more fully devoted follower of Christ, goes along with vision and its fulfillment. It must be intentional. It must involve spiritual formation, leadership development, and missional engagement.

By being involved in a disciplemaking process, not only will existing Christian disciples grow in their discipleship, but they will be a natural lifestyle witness to people they encounter in life, and some of these people will be drawn to a meaningful life as Christian disciples. Call this evangelism if you like. Or, call this attraction rather than missional. Or, call it church growth. In any case, it is an authentic overflow of a life committed to being a follower of Jesus.

Vision Insight 081: Living into vision involves congregations increasing their expectations of members and regular attendees.

As congregations live into vision they often need more lay involvement. If a cultural of vision fulfillment is flourishing in a congregation then an incremental increase of expectations of members and regular attendees will produce an increase in lay involvement.

If a culture of vision fulfillment is not flourishing it will be more difficult to increase lay involvement. The congregation may have gone through the motions of visioning without becoming positively infected by it.

Some congregational leaders are giving in to a low expectation mentality. As I was writing this section I talked with a church staff person who had decided that engaging teenagers in a service business that brings new money into his congregation was the only way they would fund their vision.

It is difficult in some situations to understand if this is giving into a low expectation of congregational financial support, or moving forward to an innovative form of ministry that has multiple benefits. What are your thoughts?

Vision Insight 082: From the Apostle Paul's life we learn that a vision of your destiny guides many choices along the road to Rome.

The Apostle Paul had a long-term, life vision of his destiny that developed after his Damascus Road experience and his Macedonian call. He responded to God's call to increase the expectations of his ministry, and knew his greatest impact would be if he could share the Good News in Rome.

He did not stop until he had fulfilled that vision. He allowed the expectations of his ministry to increase. He ministered to his full capacity. He sought to reach the full Kingdom potential God had given him.

Key Points for Your Congregation

First, once vision captivates a congregation, it becomes the fuel that drives the congregation. Everything that is done in and through the congregation must be evaluated by how effectively it helps the congregation live into God's empowering vision.

Second, the casting and celebrating of God's empowering vision is a continual action. Because vision is from God it is an important part of worship, spiritual formation, leadership development, and missional engagement.

Third, vision is not something hoarded by those who were present when it captured the spiritual imagination of the congregation. Vision must be shared with every new person who connects with the congregation. In fact, it is the significance and sacrifice of your vision that may attract them to your congregation.

Fourth, vision is a "game-changer." It raises the expectation of every disciple. Everyone is called upon to be more fervent, passionate, and committed to serving God's empowering vision.

Call to Action for Your Congregation

Develop a personal plan for how you as an individual will be part of fulfilling God's empowering vision through the life and ministry of your congregation. Determine how it will change your priorities in life, work, family, and community. Ask God to use you in ministry service through your community of believers. Figure out how and with whom you want your life to be held accountable for this new dimension of service.

George W. Bullard Jr.

A Prayer for Your Congregation

We thank you, O God, for the opportunity and challenge You have given us as a Christ-centered, faith-based community to be part of helping Your Kingdom come, and Your will be done. Search me to know how I can best serve You through this journey. Help me to see that acquiring vision was not a transaction or a project with a completion date, but a morphing and a transformation of my service to You. Amen.

CHAPTER EIGHT

Vision Renewal

Vision is always out of sight.

Northside Church completed their first generation of life, and realized their vision was beginning to wane. They were still seeking to fulfill their founder's vision that no longer applied to their situation. They were a very successful and significant congregation during their first generation. Their founding pastor was still their pastor but was close to retirement.

They engaged in a year-long process to discover God's empowering vision for the next season of their life. They did so right on time. They were twenty-something years old. Their pastor initiated the process knowing the time was right.

Many people participated in the revisioning process. Ownership was deep and wide. Ideas for future ministry were plentiful—so plentiful that the number of ideas risked smothering the clarity of the vison. They acted like they were trying to plan for the next 21 years rather than the next seven.

Because the founder's vision had waned, management was now in control. As is typical, the future was initially crafted with an overwhelming number of programs, ministries, and activities. They were literally marching off in multiple directions at once. It was way too much.

Fortunately, they recognized this in time, and embraced the idea of accomplishing more by planning to do less, which is a principle I learned from one of my mentors–Kennon Callahan. They backed up and strengthened the understanding of the vision, and then could focus on the highest priority items that would make a key difference in the ability of the congregation to serve in the midst of God's Kingdom.

They were not atypical. Many congregations plan for everything they can see. What they ought to do is plan for those things that will make the most positive impact in fulfilling their renewed vision. They should save room for what is always out of sight, and yet to be realized.

Nothing is Permanent About Congregational Vision

My father regularly said funny things about my mother. They had a healthy, loving, bantering relationship. I particularly remember one of his sayings. It was not a put-down although hyper-sensitive people might see it as that. You had to be there and experience the smiles on everyone's face when he repeated this observation.

My mother regularly went to the hair salon for a treatment called a "permanent." Although it was called a "permanent," she went every three months. Dad always said, "They ought to call it a temporary."

If there was a negative side to that saying it was because mother had run out of what was referred to as her "grocery" money, and she had to ask Dad for more money to go to the hair salon. There were days it was hard for Dad to reach into his wallet and give her that money. But he always did.

There is something in this illustration that applies to congregational vision. It is about the permanence of vision.

Vision is not permanent. It is not a one-time thing. Even the best and most empowering founding vision for a congregation only lasts about a generation. After that, vision must be renewed to acquire a new understanding that captivates the spiritual imagination of the congregation.

Renewal of a congregation's founding vision does not last for a generation. Following the first generation renewed visions only have strong, primary impact for about seven years, and then vision again must be renewed.

Since nothing is permanent about a vision, congregations who seek to institutionalize their vision discover they soon lose it. What they call vision becomes an organizational statement. It is branding at best.

No congregation can stop and rest, and say they have fulfilled their vision. What it means to be captured by a transforming vision continues to move forward. When we rejoice in our visionary action too much we begin to slow down, divert our course away from God's leading, and fall behind the cutting edge of ministry which once characterized us.

God's world is dynamic and ever-changing. We must be dynamic, ever-changing congregations who periodically renew our vision, or we slowly die. Transition and change is a continual process. What it means to be "transformed" is a moving target.

Here are three *Vision Insights* that focus more specifically on the renewal of vision as introduced above:

Vision Insight 083: The founding vision in a congregation often empowers the congregation for the first generation of its life.

Launching a new congregation is a serious Kingdom endeavor. The gestation period for a new congregation should not be shallow but deep. It should also not be too short or too long. Nine months or less is fine in many cases. In a few cases, it may take up to two years.

A sidebar note: I am framing this based on a traditional model of launching a new congregation. I am defining church as more than a fleeting Bible study or small group. On another day in another book we can dialogue about this sidebar.

If the gestation stage and the birth stage of congregations involve being captured by vision, then such a vision may last up to a generation of time, which I am suggesting is 21 years. In some cases, such as in a fast-changing context, the first generation may only be 14 to 21 years. This shorter period is generally the exception rather than the rule.

Based on this founding vision, new congregations may live out the joy of fulfilling this vision for that generation of time. Church separation groups—formerly called church splits—or congregations founded with an inadequate vision, may experience arrested development six to ten years into their life, and lose vision.

Vision Insight 084: Following the first generation of a congregation, vision must be recast, renewed, and re-owned every seven years.

A great challenge for congregations is that their founding vision from God begins to wane in its effectiveness years before the congregation both realizes it and is willing to do something about it.

When God's empowering vision begins to wane at the end of their first generation, congregations may do several things. Deny it. Try harder. Yearn to return to being the congregation they were during their early years. Look for a new programmatic fix. Blame the pastor and staff. Focus on quality rather than quantity. Become victim of the cut-back syndrome when finances get tight.

None of these attitudes or activities recast or help congregations re-own God's empowering vision for them. Plus, they create a contentious, debating culture that may involve not only decline but also dysfunction.

What congregations need to learn is that at the end of their first generation of life they need to recast, renew, and re-own God's empowering vision for them, or they will become an aging, declining, and perhaps dysfunctional congregation.

Way too many congregations become one-generation congregations who have a founding vision, live it out for a generation, and never have a new or renewed vision again. They go from fix to fix with periodic years of progress, but many years without progress.

Vision Insight 085: Even though congregational vision involves the long view during the first generation, it must still be reconceptualized thereafter at least every seven years or it starts dying.

The best congregations hardwire into their culture that once they are past their first generation they recast, renew, and re-own God's empowering vision for them every seven years. These are congregations who soar with faith decade after decade. They are the kind of congregations Robert Dale discusses in his book on *Cultivating Perennial Churches: Your Guide to Long-Term Growth* (Chalice Press 2008)

This is something congregations must own deeply. Pastors and staff transition in and out of the congregations. A key piece of congregational culture that should supersede the tenure of pastors and staff is the commitment to reconceptualize vision on a regular schedule.

The failure to reconceptualize vision can lead to a slow death march for congregations. It appears many one-generation congregations die before their 80th anniversary. Some die quicker because their context and membership transition more quickly.

If Congregational Vision is Too Clear, It May Not Be Vision

Driving along the plains in the western part of the United States and Canada, before you hit the Rocky Mountains, it looks like you can see forever. Actually, you cannot. The horizon is closer to you than you think due to the curvature of the earth. The distance between where you are at any given time and some object between you and the horizon is easily misjudged.

God's empowering vision for your congregation is beyond any horizon you see. If you see it too clearly with your eyes your vision is shortsighted. It is not likely God's empowering vision. Vision is always partially out of sight. If your congregational vision is too clear to too many people, then it may be a short-term goal rather than a long-term vision.

This is one of the challenges mentioned in a previous chapter about using new or retrofitted buildings as the object which represents vision. Buildings are all too visible, static, and management-oriented to be the vision God has for the spiritual and strategic journey of your congregation.

Congregational vision also is not a mirage. A mirage is an optical illusion caused by atmospheric conditions and related to a combination of reflected light and heated air. It appears real, but is not.

Like a mirage, vision can be a fantasy or illusion of something your congregation wants to have happen, but is unlikely, even improbable, to occur. What seems clear a few miles away as you drive along the plains, disappears the closer you get to it.

Here are three *Vision Insights* that address the issue of the clarity of vision.

Vision Insight 086: Vision, after the first generation of a congregation, expresses where a congregation discerns it will be seven years from now in response to God's leadership.

No congregation with their own gifts, skills, and preferences can accurately project where it will be almost a decade from now. There are too many unknowns. The world can present us with too many interruptions. For example, few people saw the worldwide economic crisis that was building and exploded onto the scene in 2007 and 2008. Many who should have seen it were in denial.

Yet, it is important for congregations to visualize God's empowering vision for seven years into the future. Why? Congregations need a vision that is unseen rather than one that is seen. It relates to Gideon's gang from Judges chapter 7. If congregations see and fulfill vision by their own abilities, it is likely to be their vision and not God's empowering vision.

God has a vision for each congregation they cannot see, and if they could they might be afraid of it and believe there is no way they could reach it. Only the Joshua's and Caleb's in their midst might be able at first to see the beauty and possibility of God's empowering vision.

Discerning seven years into the future, and allowing God to pull the congregation into that future, creates enough of an impossibility factor that congregations know they must depend on God for the fulfillment of vision.

Vision Insight 087: Vision will always be something beyond your current grasp, out of sight, around the corner, or over the next hill.

God's empowering vision for congregations always exists in the realm of the unseen. Congregations never arrive at the end of God's empowering vision for them. They are always running the race in the spirit of Philippians 3:12-16.

There is also a spiritual Catch-22. Whenever you think you are getting close to fulfilling God's empowering vision for your congregation, there is always another vision beyond your current reach to which God is calling you. In the spirit of Catch-22, vision fulfillment is a continual spiritual challenge. The closer you get the farther up and farther in is the destination. Vision fulfillment keeps moving forward and staying just out of sight.

By the way, for those who do not know, *Catch-22* is the title of a 1961 novel by Joseph Heller you might want to add to your reading list of classics.

Vision Insight 088: If vision is too clear it may be too short-term, not sufficiently challenging, prophetic, or focused on your full Kingdom potential.

The vision people develop is like your car's right hand mirror that reads: "Objects in this mirror are closer than they appear." If vision is too clear, too close, unchallenging, and low risk, it is not likely the vision God has for your congregation. It may be the vision you wish God would give you so you could easily achieve it, but it is not likely God's empowering vision.

It often takes a long time for congregations to arrive in a zone where they feel they are on target to fulfill God's empowering vision. Becoming prophetic and Kingdom focused is not something congregations can place on their annual calendar and check off. Consider the following church.

Southside Community Church was started about 30 years ago with the vision of reaching one percent of their metropolitan area for Christ. In their case that meant 25,000 people. During their first 30 years, they reached a weekly attendance of 4,000 in five locations, and with almost three times that many connected with the congregation. They were well on their way to fulfilling God's empowering vision.

The good news about their vision is that they talk about it all the time. They often tell stories about it. Many people recognize they have a personal part in bringing people to Christ. Their attendance in worship services, participation in small groups, missional engagement, and financial generosity are all part of vision fulfillment. They are always looking for ways to reach people with the Good News.

A key issue is how they keep God's empowering vision fresh and renew it over such a long period.

Key Points for Your Congregation

First, one of the characteristics of congregations who are continually vital and vibrant, and may always be in the *FaithSoaring* zone, is that they are agile. They anticipate every seven years a new mini-reformation whereby they redream the dream. They know vision is never permanent.

Second, one way congregations know it is time to renew their vision is when it becomes too clear, or they begin to think they have arrived. When this happens, *FaithSoaring* congregations know they need to discern the next thing God would empower in them.

Call to Action for Your Congregation

Annually send out a "Lewis and Clark Expedition" or a "Joshua and Caleb Expedition" to explore the unknown. Always be thinking, praying, and discerning the next thing God has in mind for your congregation. When the timing is right, reopen consideration of your current understanding of God's spiritual and strategic journey for your congregation, and ask God to speak into your fellowship once again.

A Prayer for Your Congregation

Precious Lord, I know we can never stop, sit down, and be satisfied that we have done enough for You. At the same time, we also know we need to rest from time-to-time to renew our energy and listen once again for Your still small voice. May we always be wondering about the next thing You are going to ask us to do. The current journey is exciting. We cannot wait to discern the next journey. Help us to be patient and to honor Your timing, O Lord. Amen.

CHAPTER NINE

Vision Killers

Those who worship the past will seek to kill vision.

I arrived at a church early to meet with the team working on financing a major building project so the congregation could handle its growth in their expanding context. I sat down in a classroom to wait for the meeting to begin.

That provided a few minutes for me to ponder the desired outcome of the meeting, and how I could help them see a way forward when they primarily see ways not to move forward. Caution reigned supreme. To a certain extent it must be present. However, it cannot be the winner if this congregation is to reach its full Kingdom potential.

There were challenges. Not everyone on the team fully believed in the project. Some saw the church as primarily a business organization and their faith went only to the end of all known and verifiable facts. They did not know how to inject the God factor into the dialogue. They had no obvious spiritual component to their perspective.

There would be more challenges. This project had already been on the table for several years. There had been some progress, and some setbacks. The growth and expansion initiative had already been around long enough that stories of the recent past dominated the conversation more than hopeful imagination about the future.

They had been captured by a great vison focused on evangelism, attracting new members, assimilating them into the congregation, developing them as believers, and engaging them in missional action. But did they truly believe in their vision? Could their unbelief kill their vision?

Congregational Vision is Never a Journey Back Home

Some people are vision killers. They are the crazies that keep your congregation from reaching your full Kingdom potential. Vision killers are unwilling to change, and they celebrate more where you have been than they are inspired about where you are going. They focus on familiar members with longer tenure without also balancing those friendships with seeking to engage the next generation in the journey.

Vision killers focus on short-term fixes that repeat the way you've always done them, rather than long-term solutions that are willing to stretch in new directions where God is leading you. Vision killers are culturally captive to ways of understanding congregational ministry, rather than being spiritual risk takers seeking prophetic pathways.

Vision killers often lack passion about the future toward which God is leading their congregation. Their lack of passion may express itself as passive or active resistance. They may never have thought of themselves as protest demonstrators marching in the street, but that is figuratively what they are doing.

They express their resistance with a lack of positive, powerful praying for the future of the congregation. They speak negative words about their congregation to others. They decrease their level of activity, and withhold or designate their tithes and offerings. Often they oppose the leadership of the pastor and staff.

Vision killers are hoping tomorrow will bring a return of yesterday. They see the best journey as a trip back home to safe, familiar, and successful territory. Unfortunately, they be oblivious to the cliché that "the good old days were neither."

Here are three *Vision Insights* that highlight various aspects of vision killers:

Vision Insight 089: Vision is about leaving your land of heritage and going forward to a new place God will show you as was experienced by Abram in Genesis 12:1-4.

Congregational vision, because it is from God and is about the future, and responds to the call of God to go forth to a new place of dwelling. It is not necessarily about moving to a new physical location, but it is about going on a spiritual and strategic journey in response to God's call.

It usually does involve a leaving. Congregations must be willing to leave their current place in their spiritual and strategic journey, and serve in new dimensions of ministry.

In leaving, congregations are not asked to forget their heritage, but to use their heritage as a foundation for what's next in their journey. Heritage can be remembered, appreciated, and acted on as a starting point to engage in new and prophetic ministry that fulfills God's empowering vision.

Vision killers may want their congregation to be reimaged in their image. But only God's image is sufficient.

Vision Insight 090: People with vision know they must leave the 99 and focus on the one. People without vision primarily see the 99. We are challenged on this in Luke 15:14.

Typically, congregations at least a generation old tend to focus more on the 99 connected with them than those who are not. Unfortunately, they come across as anti-missional and anti-evangelism. They likely did not adopt this attitude intentionally. They believe faithfulness by longer tenured and older people should be rewarded. This is their congregation and they want to be served.

They become vision killers. They especially have a hard time with vision focused on those who are outside the congregation. They have forgotten that congregations primarily exist for people who are not church members and are not Christians.

Vision Insight 091: Vision involves forgetting what is behind, and looking forward to what is ahead as urged in Philippians 3:13.

Congregations captured by God's empowering vision are willing, in the spirit of Philippians 3:13ff, to forget what is behind and reach forward to what is ahead, to press on for the prize of the upward call of God in Christ Jesus. They see vision as a forward journey. They see life in Christ as an invaluable reason to move forward.

Vision killers believe such an attitude abandons the heritage of the congregation. They believe buildings, programs, and significant historic and spiritual events in the life of the church cannot be abandoned. One wonders if the people are pleased and excited about the possibility of living an eternity with the Triune God, or if they would prefer things the way they once were in their life, family, work, and church.

Vision killers are afraid they will never be able to go home again. Their fear is well founded. They will not be able to go back once they allow God to pull them forward in fulfillment of a captivating, empowering vision. What they don't realize, is that they would not want to go back.

Congregational Vision Does Not Destroy the Past or Ignore Heritage

Congregational vision is not opposed to the past. It does not see the past as bad, or as something to destroy. It is not trying to rewrite history. It is appropriately proud of heritage. God was present and active during the heritage years of congregations. God is present and active now. God wants to draw congregations into a future of reaching their full Kingdom potential.

It is just that congregational vision favors the future. It prefers to allow God to draw them forward toward their full Kingdom potential.

The oldest congregation I have had the privilege to come alongside as a strategic leadership coach is more than 325 years old. They are very proud of their past. They have a right to be. Some of their pride refers to things that happened 300 years ago. Yet, at the same time they have an and/both perspective on the future. They respect and honor their heritage, and they move enthusiastically towards their God-given future. That is how it ought to be.

Vision Insight 092: Vision is always about the future, never about the past. The past is a prelude to the emerging future.

Congregational vision is never about going back to the past. It is always going forward to the future. I tell congregations one four-letter word to eliminate from their speech is the word "back." While our God is the God of the past, present, and future, I believe God celebrates when congregations become more Christ-like and are more prophetically involved in missional engagement with a future consequence.

The past does have an important role to play in the future. It is prelude to the future worship of the Triune God as we live into God's empowering vision.

Prelude is not just that music played before the worship service begins, while people are still visiting with one another, the choir or praise band is getting in place, or a countdown clock on screens is letting you know visiting time is short. Prelude is what happens before actions of a deeper scope or high importance begin to take place.

Vision Insight 093: Vision does not call for the rejection of heritage. It sees heritage as a foundation, a centering, and a mooring.

Heritage provides a foundation. For example, the substance of worship, such as who congregations worship and why, never changes. We always worship the Triune God. That is not open for negotiation. Congregations are not planning to worship a popular entertainer, actor, politician, or other persons of notoriety.

I did once visit a church on the west coast of the United States that had persons of notoriety painted on the ceiling and they danced around in a circle celebrating these people. Let's not go there today.

Our theology, which is our substance, gives us a centering and mooring about our long-term commitments as a congregation. It is when this centering changes that congregations and denominations split, or separate into multiple parts, and vision becomes confused.

Vision Insight 094: Vision which is not fulfilled in new and innovative ways each year will become stale and lose its cutting edge.

As empowering as it is to be captured by God's vision, that vision does not come with a playbook for living into it. New and innovative methods for living into the vision still must be crafted annually. Recruit the most passionate and creative people in your congregation, who are committed to continual innovation, to help navigate the way forward.

There still will be resistance to change. This will come particularly from people who cannot see or accept new methodologies. No one ever told them they would have to change.

They also may never have affirmed the congregational vision and its future story of ministry. So, they feel no ownership. They kill vision. They feel justified in resisting change to old ways they find acceptance and comfort.

When congregational vision becomes stale, that does not always mean vision is gone. It may only mean ownership and excitement surrounding vision has drifted away. It may be possible to reactivate this ownership and refocus the vision.

Vision Insight 095: When vision wanes in congregations they can become angry at God for forsaking them, when they may actually have forsaken God.

Congregational vision does not move forward on auto-pilot. Congregational participants must believe in the vision sufficiently to be part of God's empowering force. When vision wanes within a congregation, then it is not being cast assertively, movement toward its fulfillment is not a high enough priority within the congregation, or the congregation has become distracted and lost its focus. Vision killers love to distract their congregation.

God does not forsake God's empowering vision for a congregation. Congregations forsake God's empowering vision. Anger is never a great response. Perhaps as close as a congregation ought to come to anger would be the concept known as "righteous indignation."

During the second and following generations of a congregation, when vision wanes in less than seven years, congregations need to recalibrate and move forward. When vision wanes at or after seven years, it may be time to go through a season of renewing vision. If a congregation does not renew vision within ten years since its last vision was cast, it is likely to become aging, declining, and perhaps even dysfunctional.

Congregational Vision Seldom Comes from Long-Tenure Members

Tenure is a key factor in congregational vision. The longer people have related to a congregation, the less likely they are to live on the innovative edge with those who easily embrace new vision.

It does not mean they will not actively embrace vision. It's just that they are less likely to be on the innovative edge of leadership. They are more likely to prefer incremental transitions and changes that do not significantly alter the character and nature of the congregation. They are more comfortable with things the way they are. They will at times embrace short-term fixes. If pushed too hard or fast, they may seek to kill vision.

Do not confuse tenure with age. Don't think it is necessarily "the old people" who are holding the congregation back. While this may seem to be true, it is not true. The key variable could be tenure.

I have contended for years that a 72-year-old recently widowed woman who moves to your area to be close to her children and grandchildren, and then connects with your congregation is more open to transition and change then a 30-something person who has been attending your congregation since birth.

Vision Insight 096: In general, the longer people are connected with a congregation, the more difficult it is to see a new vision.

The routine patterns and habits within the fellowship of a congregation blind people to new vision. In older churches, there is a group of people I call 60-40-20 people. They are at least 60 years old, have been in church at least 40 years, and have been attending your church at least 20 years. This is a cohort for whom it is almost impossible to see new vision.

They are also overly churched culture people. They have difficulty being led to see new vision by people of a short tenure. They cannot speak the language of the unchurched culture. They can only speak the language of the churched culture.

They know the language of Zion and the secret handshake, and do not understand why non-churched people might think that hymns with the word "blood" in them are talking about some form of cannibalism, vampires, or perhaps zombies.

They still understand highway signs that suggest people are going to hell without Jesus. They do not realize the next generation of pre-Christians do not understand the signs, and if they did, they would be driven away rather than attracted.

Vision Insight 097: Killers of a new vision in a congregation are the people who will not let go of the old vision that has waned.

Long-tenured members who will not let go of a waning vision worship what was. They add heritage as the fourth person of the Trinity.

As Lyle Schaller said, "You can tell the old-timers from the newcomers at the church fellowship. The old-timers sit around the campfire telling lies about the past, and the newcomers do not understand the stories." The old-timers are stuck on their image of the congregation of the past. The newcomers are looking for a fresh approach to faith and spiritual significance.

I am one of those older adults who likes traditional worship with some liturgical highlights. At the same time, I want my congregation to employ styles of worship that connect with younger generations. Can I have both? If so, I can give permission for a vision that grasps an emerging future, even as I reluctantly release the old vision that is waning.

Vision Insight 098: Myopia prohibits many long-tenured congregational members from seeing the long-term benefits of new vision.

Many longer-tenured members are nearsighted. They are myopic. Part of this may be their age. They are thinking in shorter life stages. They're not sure they should buy green bananas.

Just as they want to conserve principal and not take risks with their retirement funds, they are not open to a bold new vision for their congregation. They would prefer to preserve the accomplishments of their congregation, pay off any existing debt and certainly not take on any new risks.

I have tried many ways to unfreeze these people in congregations. The most successful question I have asked that gets them to reframe their position is, "What would you be willing to change to make this the kind of congregation your grandchildren would want to attend?"

Vision Insight 099: God's empowering vision often disrupts the status quo and who is in charge. That is why some people try to kill it.

Many vision killers want to retain their positions of power. They may even want to control all the decision-making. Because crafting vision focuses on people with positive spiritual passion more than it does on people with elected or appointed positions, they do not trust the vision.

Rick Smyre, a futurist and long-term friend, has said the most conservative thing a congregation's governance group can do is to change something. If they control the change, then after the change is made they are still in control. If they cannot be in control, then they will kill the vision.

Vision Insight 100: Vision is more about transformation of the prodigals than honoring the elders among us.

Congregational vision is more about creating a congregation not only in tune with God's leadership, but with a structure and style that will connect with the next generation of leaders. With deep and abiding appreciation for the older people in a congregation, we must realize vision is more about captivating the imagination of the younger generations.

Some younger generation people are prodigals in the sense that they may still be going through their 20-somethings spiritual wanderings. Reconnecting with church is still a future agenda for them. In many cases, it is this Millennial generation who are the crucial clients for the new congregational vision. They want to be part of a cause that both speaks to their need for community while simultaneously changing the world.

If the older generations cannot let go enough, then they may kill vision. If they refuse to let God's new empowering vision for the emerging generations develop, they will eventually kill the congregation.

Vision Insight 101: When the first century church at Jerusalem lost vision and slowed missional action, it invented the holy huddle. Now many congregations follow their example and hoard the Good News.

The biggest vision killer is when congregations lose vision and huddle. They fear failing more than being open to joyously fulfilling God's empowering vision for them. They focus more on taking care of one another than they do on caring for those most in need of a Christ-centered, faith-based relationship in their lives.

Out of guilt, obedience, or a sense of duty they engage in what I call "detached" missional engagement. It is detached from the full ministry of the congregation. They do not expect to be sitting next to the people to whom they minister during the week when they worship on Sunday.

This is missional engagement where congregations perform a ministry service either to or at people they never see otherwise. There is no attempt at holistic ministry that deals with physical, social, and emotional needs as well as spiritual needs.

Congregations gathered in holy huddle have difficulty ever seeing Jesus as the embodiment of God's empowering vision for them. They age, slowly decline, and at some point become dysfunctional. They hoard good news rather than sow the Good News.

Key Points for Your Congregation

First, there will always be groups of people in your congregation who never get it about vision. They will wonder about—even oppose—the new things happening because they do not get it nor understand it. Remember to count the "yes" votes more than you count the "no" votes.

Second, along the journey, always honor and respect the past. Acknowledge the real spiritual and emotional struggles of the present, but never take your eye off the prize of the high calling of God in Christ Jesus that is represented in vision fulfillment.

Third, figuratively put your ear to the ground to hear what your recent new members are saying. Because they are experiencing the congregation without the baggage of the past, they may be the ones who most clearly see the implications of God's empowering vision.

Call to Action for Your Congregation

Listening is an important part of living into the vision. It is a crucial way to keep vision killers from derailing vision fulfillment. Intentionally find ways to listen both to long-term and short-term members, to older members and younger members, to people who once held leadership roles in the congregation as well as people new to leadership. The spiritual and emotional expressions of all people are important. People want to be heard and understood. No one wants to feel like someone stole their church.

A Prayer for Your Congregation

Gracious God, we believe we have clearly heard Your voice and responded to Your empowering vision. But, not everyone is with us—with You. Yet there are still many persons of worth in our congregation created in Your image to live and to love. Help us to be community. Help us to be in fellowship with one another and You. Amen.

CHAPTER TEN

Getting from Here to Vision

If one does not know to which port one is sailing, no wind is favorable.
--Seneca, Roman philosopher

Getting from where you are to being captured by God's empowering vision is not an easy journey. It is not a journey on a straight road. It is chaordic with a combination of chaos and order. It is a spiritual and strategic journey. It is more about experiences than statements. It is a focus on the Triune God as the source of vision.

What happens when congregations have gone too long without being captured by God's empowering vision? They often struggle against engaging in a process that would help them to be captured by vision.

Many people have their own idea as to what needs to happen for the congregation to move forward. They do not necessarily accept initiatives of current leaders because they don't trust these people to take them forward into a future they personally envision for their congregation.

Such was the case with the Church of the Redeemer. Throughout a medium length pastorate of 10 to 12 years there were regular calls for the congregation to take a hard look at their situation, and project a more robust future. I am not sure this congregation saw God as the source of vision. Some controlling persons saw themselves as the source.

A new pastor came to the congregation. He realized immediately the congregation needed a new sense of God's vision, and proactive strategies to live into that vision.

The church entered a year-long process to become captured once again by God's empowering vision. Significant numbers of people participated in the process—but not members of the group that wanted to control the future direction of the congregation. They wanted a different direction and they had little confidence the new pastor would lead them there.

Despite a powerful and positive process, a small group of long-term influential people withheld their affirmation. They not only withheld their personal support for the new direction, they decreased their attendance, opposed specific strategies and tactics, and withheld their financial support.

Because of this, it took the congregation several years for the new vision to gain traction. Getting from here to vision involves deep and abiding commitment to live into the vision. Even with an open and broadly owned process, some people still could not see Jesus. In this case, it was people able to hold the congregation hostage until the power of vision finally overcame their opposition.

Looking at another congregation, what happens when sufficient confusion about vision arises within a congregation or they institutionalize around their way of doing church way too soon? While they are not at least 21 years old, they may still need to find a new entry point to becoming captured by God's empowering vision.

For Crossroad Community Church it meant an earlier than typical re-envisioning process. What they were doing had stopped working. They recognized they were plateaued so they sought outside assistance, and began working their way through a new visioning process.

Ultimately it involved their becoming a marketplace congregation. They moved from an inadequate physical site into the facilities of a suburban YMCA in an upper middle class community. The "Y" had the room, the technology, the parking, and the programs that fit what the congregation needed to do to interact with households in their community setting. Their vision of reaching their community happened not by inviting people to come to their church facility, but by going to where people gathered and offering them the unconditional love of the Triune God.

Unlike the Church of Redeemer that needed many years to refocus their vision, Crossroads Community Church went from here to vision within a year or so. Where they ended up—both in their vision and their physical location—was not where the re-envisioning process first took them. It involved God opening doors they never thought would be available to them. Truly God was the source of the new vision.

To Which Port Are You Sailing?

Ray Rust is one of the most genuine, kind, and effective leaders I ever had the privilege to know. He was the executive director and my supervisor at the South Carolina Baptist Convention in Columbia, SC for seven years before he retired. He is the one who hired me. He is still alive at this writing, is closing in on 90 years old, and thoughts of his leadership, character, and personality still inspire me.

He carried a small date book around in his coat pocket. In that date book he had written the quote from Seneca which is found at the beginning of this chapter. When he was leading the staff, our board, or a group of leaders in a discussion on focus, direction, and planning, he would pull that date book out and read the saying of Seneca.

This is a simple, yet extremely important statement for congregations struggling with whether to pursue God's empowering vision, and if so, how to go about becoming captured by it. Way too many congregations do not know the port toward which they are sailing, and what adjustments to their sails they should make to catch the winds which could carry them there.

Who Wants God's Empowering Vision?

How does a congregation get from here to vision? There are multiple pathways. Learning which one will work for your congregation is an important point of readiness for vision. Here are various starting places.

New Congregations: Many new congregations launched by various methods have a clear understanding of the port toward which they are sailing. Those who are separation groups—formerly called church splits, or new congregations trying to emulate or function as a franchise or satellite of another successful congregation, are seldom launched with a deeply empowering vision from God.

Congregations Not Open to God's Empowering Vision: Congregations who are at least a generation old are a more difficult story. Forty years of working with these congregations indicates six out of ten congregations at least a generation old are not interested in a new vision unless it is one that magically transforms them without changing anything.

Congregations Who Want Vision Without Significant, Discontinuous Change: The next two out of ten congregations are interested in new vision if it does not significantly change the character and nature of their congregation. They are interested in short-term fixes rather than long-term solutions. They have difficulty realigning what they do to fulfill vision. They may want vision without having to stop doing old things they love, and start doing new things of which they are unsure. They may fail to achieve true vision plus intentionality because their resistance to change is too high.

Congregations Desiring Vision Plus Intentionality: The final two out of ten congregations are interested in a new, empowering vision from God, and realize they must be open to deep transition and change that leads to transformation. They also realize they must be willing to repeat this process every seven years.

Not only are they willing to be captured by God's empowering vision, they are willing to reconceptualize their programs, ministries, activities, governance, finances, and staff to fulfill vision. They are the ones who stand the best chance of achieving vision plus intentionality.

I know two out of ten is not encouraging. Ways exist to improve these percentages. These figures are not fatalistic, yet they represent the long-term pattern. Changing these percentages relates to readiness.

Readiness for Vision

The biggest challenge for congregations about getting from here to vision is their lack of readiness. They want the journey from being at rest to being fully captured by new vision to be one highly effective, short-term step. They fail to understand what it takes.

They want instant vision, but that does not typically happen. They want their senior or solo pastor to magically inspire them about a new vision, whether or not it is from God. They want to incorporate the next great program offered by their denomination, or a parachurch group, or a vision that has worked for a mega church nearby or far away.

It is just not that easy. From my decades of experience, I found there are five readiness factors congregations must achieve before efforts at discerning God's empowering vision will be successful and lasting. That is, short of God's "Triple D" which I say is the direct, dramatic, divine intervention of God.

I cover four of these factors more extensively than I do here in chapter two of my earlier book entitled *Pursuing the Full Kingdom Potential of Your Congregation* (Chalice Press, 2005).

1. **Urgency Readiness:** For congregations to be captured by God's empowering vision there must be a sense of positive, prophetic urgency about a goal toward which God is pulling the congregation. It is not a negative dissatisfaction with things the way they are. It is a positive sense God is up to something in and through the

congregation, and a spiritual and strategic journey fueled by vision plus intentionality is essential to realizing this.

Negative urgency is for congregations who want to fix what is wrong with them. Positive urgency is for congregations who desire to soar with faith into a future toward which God is pulling them.

2. **Spiritual Readiness:** Congregations are a spiritual organism. As such, they move forward from a spiritual foundation toward a spiritual destination. As a spiritual organism, they must seek God's guidance for vision. Some type of spiritual process must help congregational participants get ready for the new thing God is seeking to do through them.

A spiritual readiness exercise or season will help congregational participants become ready for transition and change that can lead to transformation. Spiritual organisms must launch spiritual and emotional transition before they are ready for change.

3. **Leadership Readiness:** In several places in this book I've referenced the necessity of 21 percent of the average number of adults present on a typical weekend for worship as the benchmark of participation for acquiring God's empowering vision. This is the number necessary to secure leadership readiness. This is the minimum number of people who must engage in a spiritual readiness exercise.

In congregations where these are less than 100 adults present weekly for worship, which is most congregations, the raw number of 21 adults is the benchmark. This is regardless of how much less than 100 adults are present during a typical week. Implied in this statement is that a congregation with less than 21 adults present for weekly worship, where the congregation is also at least a generation old, may not be able to both experience new vision and have the leadership to live into that vision.

4. **Strategic Readiness:** Congregations must have strategic knowledge of the past, present, and potential future of their congregation, and of their community context, to be ready to understand the vision God will seek to impart to them. Awareness and knowledge of internal and external demographics is essential to understand the framework for vision.

   Congregations must also have an effective pattern of annual planning and actions so they have a foundation for living into their vision. Some congregations need to engage in annual planning and implementation actions for a year or two before they are ready to receive vision that will look at a seven-year horizon.

   Strategic readiness is basically about a proven track record of regular, ongoing planning and action that is successful and perhaps significant in adding quality, and even quantity, to the life of the congregation. A congregation that does not plan does not have consistent actions that add value to its life. They cannot go from zero to proactive overnight.

5. **Resource Readiness:** What are the resources available to live into God's empowering vision? What are the assets in place or available to the congregation that can be applied to living into God's empowering vision? A congregation must have leadership, facilities, governance, finances, equipment, and materials of various types they can use to engage in the programs, ministries, and activities that will flow out of a discerned vision.

   With readiness handled, what are the various pathways for getting from here to vision?

Pathways to God's Empowering Vision

I have observed six pathways whereby congregations become captured by God's empowering vision. These are Founder's Pathway, Hastened Pathway, Sabbath Pathway, Kairos Pathway, Chronos Pathway, and Empowering Pathway. Would you suggest any others?

Founder's Pathway: Founder's pathway happens when there is no one other than the founding pastor of a congregation with whom God can work to bring forth an empowering vision for the new congregation. At first it may be only the founder and his or her household. Through prayer, study, and observation the founder concludes God desires a new congregation to be launched in a certain geographic location or among a certain affinity group.

The founder at first is the only one who owns the vision. Casting the vision to everyone the founder encounters in conversation is a key role. It is a great example of the pastor being the voice of God's empowering vision and giving the vision away to others so they may own it, help craft the casting of vision, and certainly to take actions to fulfill vision.

The Founder's Pathway is a unique experience for congregations, and I suggest it never occurs again in the life of a congregation. Wise founders understand God's empowering vision is something they hold in sacred trust for the congregation that may emerge and deeply own the vision. It is not a vision for them alone.

Founders gather followers of God's empowering vision into a congregational community. In doing so they give vision away and allow God to work through the congregation. This can be difficult for some founders to handle. Their desire to control the focus and actions of the congregation, and to lay claim to the vision as one God primarily gave to them. This is a difficult barrier for many founders to overcome.

How the vision for new congregations is formed depends a lot on the model used to start new congregations. I have observed three primary models. First, is the model of an existing congregation starting a new congregation as a missional extension of its overall ministry. In these cases, the sponsoring congregation may form the initial vision for the new congregation out of the overflow of their own congregational ministry.

Second is where the founding vision emerges from a demographic study of geography or the affinity group that is the focus of a new congregation. Third is where the founding vision is developed out of the spiritual passion of the persons launching the new congregation. What is the initial vision God has given them that they must share? This third model best fits the founder's vision concept, and appears to be the one most popular in North America now.

I personally was the founder of three congregations during my early ministry. All three were seeking to reach families and households in a certain geographical area. It was essential in each case for the congregations to reflect the spiritual and cultural needs of the people in their setting.

Hastened Pathway: Hastened or accelerated pathway happens by a "ready, shoot, aim" approach. This is when some opportunity or challenge arises that causes a congregation to work quickly on a new vision. They need God's empowering vision or they cannot move forward and take the next steps with assurance they are acting in response to God's leadership.

An open window of opportunity has given them only a short period to get a focus. Perhaps God is already working within their fellowship to clarify vision, but the congregation is not engaged in an intentional process.

One time I was asked to work with a congregation that was thinking about restructuring staff in line with their future needs. They wanted to look at various innovative models as to how to staff a large, growing congregation. I asked for some basic information, including a copy of any long-range or strategic plan.

Their last formal plan was about ten years old. Since then a fast-growing university in their town was transforming the size and culture of their area. The church was now out of building and parking space. When I arrived, I discovered they also had a building committee that was getting ready to contract with an architect to draw plans for increasing their facilities footprint.

I began asking simple questions about the clarity of God's empowering vision over the next ten years that would drive a new staff structure and guide construction of facilities. No one had asked these simple questions. They were driven by the fact they were behind and needed to catch up.

They wanted buildings and staffing for what had happened to them over the past ten years rather than what God might do in and through them for the next ten years.

They panicked realizing they were about to move forward on staffing and facilities without a clear sense of where God was leading them next, and what capacities they might need in facilities and staffing. The great news was they had a sense of positive urgency that motivated them to be open to God's empowering vision.

A sense of positive urgency should not be taken lightly. It is such a difficult thing for many congregations to acquire, that when you experience it, you are experiencing a thing of great beauty.

With this foundation, we could fast-track a process of crafting a future story for the life and ministry of this congregation. To do this they set aside everything they could and gave priority focus to this effort. They were motivated. They saw the value of the process. They desired God's empowering vision.

We used a quick process of developing three scenarios about their future. The congregation chose one that appeared to be where God was leading them, and then crafted a future story of ministry. This desired future became the vision off which they did some very successful and significant work over the next ten years.

This quick vision approach only works when all five factors of readiness are present. This congregation had urgency readiness, spiritual readiness, leadership readiness, strategic readiness, and resource readiness.

Many congregations want a quick fix. Few are ready for it. Many congregations try for a quick fix. Few are successfully pulled forward into God's empowering future because of it.

Sabbath Pathway: Sabbath pathway happens when a congregation has been working hard for many years seeking to be successful, and then decides they need to take a time of sabbath to be sure what they are doing is significant in God's eyes and involves a surrender to God's will. Ideally a sabbath is every seven years.

Perhaps the congregation has overachieved in programs, staffing, or facilities development. It may have also focused on attractional ministry or church growth rather than missional or incarnational ministry. It may have had unrealistic numerical goals that were not from God, and created a culture that was not sufficiently holy and then became dysfunctional.

They now realize they need to be still for a while and allow God to speak to them about going deeper with the quality of their ministry. They need more evidence of empowering people to become fully devoted followers of Christ and not just good church members. Successful ministry is often about the congregation. Significant ministry is usually about disciplemaking. Surrender is always about being fully devoted followers of Christ.

Further, they may have burned out both their clergy and lay leadership, and need to figure out why they work so hard to reach goals and fulfill a vision that seems more from humankind than from God. As I write this the pastor of a multi-site church whose goal was having 100,000 people worshiping each weekend in the various locations, but could not consistently break 40,000, is in a residential treatment center for his abuse of alcohol. Possibly a forced sabbath may allow him to rethink God's empowering vision for his life and his ministry.

Congregations may also focus on a sabbath vision when they experienced a major crisis some years earlier, and worked hard to get beyond those years of turmoil. Or, perhaps they faced the crisis of decline and aging, and worked hard for many years on not dying. Now they are ready once again to be vital and vibrant.

Congregations need to realize the words of the Lord to the sons of Israel through Moses at Mount Sinai: "Six years you shall sow your field, and six years you shall prune your vineyard and gather in its crop, but during the seventh year the land shall have a sabbath rest, a sabbath to the Lord; you shall not sow your field nor prune your vineyard. Your harvest's aftergrowth you shall not reap, and your grapes of untrimmed vines you shall not gather; the land shall have a sabbatical year." (Leviticus 25:3-5 NASB)

During the sabbath year congregations need to stop doing as many programs, ministries, and activities as possible. They must take a year to listen to the Lord and be filled with a fresh expression of God's Spirit in their individual lives, and their life and ministry as a congregation.

Sabbath vision is a maturing process for congregations. It allows them to choose wisely how they go about fulfilling God's empowering vision. It is about deciding what is truly important, and what is just busy work to fulfill personal and cultural expectations.

Kairos Pathway: Kairos pathway happens when without warning, probably at some hinge point or major incident in the life of a congregation, or through some type of spiritual awakening, a clear, empowering vision from God becomes obvious. It represents an "Ah ha!" experience for congregations who may say in response, "So, that is God's empowering vision for us."

Generally, a kairos pathway, a unique visitation of God's empowering vision, would not have been realized had it not been for some incident that caused congregational leaders to see their life and ministry situation from a different perspective. Something produced a discontinuous or radical change, and during it the congregation heard with their heart, soul, mind, and strength the voice of God speaking to them in a fresh way.

Despite everything I have said in this book, many congregational leaders would prefer if God would simply "Record the vision And inscribe it on tablets, That the one who reads it may run." (Habakkuk 2:2 KJV) An alternate interpretation in the NASB reads, "the one who is to proclaim it may run." This latter seems to best fit the role of the pastor as vision caster.

If this is your hope, I have some great news for you. At times the Triune God appears to do this. The only challenge is that we do not know when and where. We cannot call down fire from heaven to make it happen. It just happens.

When it happens, it does not necessarily mean God's empowering vision is totally clear. It may mean something happens where it is obvious this experience is the opportunity and empowerment for new vision. Or, leaders have an "Ah ha!" experience that helps them see something that is speaking clearly about God's empowering vision.

Perhaps a disappointment even in these times is that the Holy Grail of a succinct vision statement still does not emerge out of these situations. As if that was the desired thing to have any way. It still means congregations must work out the clarity and actions of their vision with fear and trembling.

I once worked with a congregation seeking to acquire new vision within a limited time schedule because they were running out of money. They had enough money to last them about two to three years between their current income and their reserves. They were spending their reserves at a fast pace.

They had already closed half of their building, and were seeking to rent it to an outside tenant. They had begun discussing a plan to downsize staff to a pastor, and a couple of other essential part-time positions.

The congregation had a lot of good qualities. They were diverse racially, ethnically, and socioeconomically. They were reasonably reflective of their transitional urban area. At the same time, they were having difficulty focusing on an empowering vision of what God was calling them to do.

During this time, they were approached by an immigrant group from Asia who had been evangelized by missionaries from their own denomination. Would this congregation allow the immigrant congregation to meet in their facilities?

From the start this was a no-brainer. It was a grace gift of God. Rather than inviting the immigrant congregation to just meet within their facilities, they invited them to integrate into the congregation bringing their full gifts, skills, and preferences with them.

It was an opportunity for instant vision. The two congregations carefully and prayerfully worked their way through appropriate fellowship experiences and conversations as a new, empowering vision from God emerged that allowed them to be one congregation.

While this did not immediately solve the financial challenges, it was a new beginning. It was a kairos moment that was realized, and built upon.

Chronos Pathway: Chronos pathway happens when congregations decide it is time to address the issue of God's empowering vision once again in the life of their congregations. There are two perspectives on a chronos vision.

The first is when the calendar says it is time to do long-range or strategic planning again, whether a congregation needs to or not. Often this comes from a management perspective and may lead to a transactional process of renewing vision.

I partially, but not fully, support this perspective in one sense. It is that after a congregation completes its first generation of life, the vision inevitably wanes. It may also not be as relevant as it was a generation earlier when the congregation was founded. I always recommend to congregations once they are a generation old to hardwire into their culture that every seven years thereafter they engage in an intentional process to renew their ownership of God's empowering vision, including being open to their vision changing significantly.

This is not the same as declaring the calendar says the congregation must engage in a new futuring process now. The understanding of the need to renew vision is a right-brained relational process, and not a left-brained task. Chronos is more about when it feels right than when the calendar says it is right.

I recall hearing management guru Jim Collins talk about the difference between telling time and building clocks. Chronos vision can turn into telling time. At its best it should be about building clocks.

In my Baptist tribe, there was a great gathering of Baptists in 2008 called the New Baptist Covenant. Between 15,000 and 20,000 people were present in Atlanta for this gathering. Former President Jimmy Carter was the inspiration and key visionary for the gathering,

Three years later President Carter wanted to do it again. The second gathering was much less successful than the first. In the lead up to the event the more than 30 Baptist-related organizations who had supported the first gathering, lacked the same passion that had existing around the 2008 gathering.

One national denominational leader said, as pressure was coming for everyone to get on-board with the second gathering, that the first gathering seemed like a kairos moment. The second gathering, however, seemed like a chronos moment. The same magic was not there. This can also happen with congregations who tell time rather than build clocks.

The second perspective on chronos vision happens when intuitively it is felt that the strength of God's empowering vision is waning, and it is time to discern it once again. Often this comes from a leadership perspective and may lead to transformational process of renewing vision. The best chronos vision efforts may result in a kairos moment, although they seldom start out that way.

Empowering Pathway: Empowering pathway happens when a congregation is without vision, or knows its vision has waned, and it needs a deep, meaningful process of discovering or rediscovering God's empowering vision for them.

It is not uncommon for the demographics within a congregation and its geographic community to shift. When this happens congregations must re-own their understanding of God's spiritual and strategic direction for them for the current and future times.

It is on these occasions that I recommend congregations embark on a one-year Spiritual Strategic Journey briefly explained here. The purpose of a Spiritual Strategic Journey process is to empower a congregational journey that is both spiritual and strategic in nature, and moves them in the direction of their full Kingdom potential. They are pulled forward by God's future story of ministry for them as a congregation on mission. The goal is to live into their future story of ministry as a congregational movement.

Readiness is mandatory. Before the Spiritual Strategic Journey process can begin a congregation must determine their readiness, willingness, and commitment to engage in the process.

A Spiritual Strategic Journey process has three seasons: *Spiritual Season, Strategic Season,* and *Journey Season.* Each season lasts around 120 days, although the journey is only the beginning. Journey is the ongoing aspect of the Spiritual Strategic Journey process.

- *Spiritual Season for Transitioning*: This season is about transition in the relationship of the congregation with God, one another, and the context in which the congregation serves. The primary activity is 100 Days of Discernment using Dialogue and Prayer Triplets.
- *Strategic Season for Changing*: This season is about determining the changes that need to be made. The primary activity is crafting the Future Story of Ministry for the congregation.
- *Journey Season for Transforming*: This season is about taking the journey in the direction of God's full Kingdom potential for your congregation. The primary activities are developing the Future Story Fulfillment Map and beginning to live into the Future Story of Ministry.

The outcome of the Spiritual Strategic Journey process is a dynamic Future Story of Ministry of what will characterize the congregation ten years into the future, a Future Story Fulfillment Map that is an operational plan for the first one to three years, and a congregation committed to live into their Future Story of Ministry.

The impact of the Spiritual Strategic Journey process is not only clarity of direction and a purposeful future, but congregational leadership committed to living into that direction, and proactively aligning the programs, ministries, and activities of the congregation to fulfill the Future Story of Ministry.

Key Points for Your Congregation

First, not every congregation who says they want a new empowering vision from God, is willing to engage in the process to acquire it, and to embrace the transitions and changes it will require.

Second, few congregations are ready for a new empowering vision from God the day they say they want one. Congregations must be willing to assess their readiness around the five key factors.

Third, there are multiple pathways to God's empowering vision. The six suggested here are not an exhaustive list of how and when to become captured by God's empowering vision.

Call to Action for Your Congregation

Begin a discernment process to determine if your congregation desires to be captured by God's empowering vision. Assess your congregation with challenging criteria around the five readiness factors. Seek to discern, based on your congregational relationship with the Triune God, which pathway to vision best describes your situation. Secure any assistance needed from a consultant, coach, or other third-party provider to congregations.

A Prayer for Your Congregation

God of the past, present, and future, lead us forward in the direction You desire for us. Help us to patiently discern Your leading, Your goal for us, and what life will be like when we are captured by Your empowering vision. Help us to come to a place where we realize the full Kingdom potential You have for our congregation. May we without hesitation be willing to surrender all we are and have to live into that potential. With great anticipation we pray. Amen.

Afterword

Call to Action

I call on your congregation to be captured by God's empowering vision. God is calling your congregation to reach its full Kingdom potential. To do this, to soar with faith, you must be willing to discern, discover, and develop fulfillment actions around your understanding of God's spiritual and strategic direction for your congregation. Then you must have a deep commitment to live into, to fulfill, and to celebrate your journey as God pulls your congregation forward.

I call on you as the senior or solo pastor of a congregation, as a staff person, as a lay leader, as a person with positive spiritual passion about the future of the congregation toward which God is pulling you to be part of an *Enduring Visionary Leadership Community* which acts as a guiding coalition for the spiritual and strategic journey of your congregation.

Consider These Questions:

What new understandings have you developed from reading these 101 insights to empower your congregation to be captured by vision? How do you need to transition and change your approach to the development, casting, and fulfillment of vision? In what ways are you already on target?

Did you pick up any ideas about how to develop vision in your congregation? What did you see in these insights you could use to become captured by God's empowering vision?

Do you have a personal vision for your life and ministry? I suspect leaders who are clear about vision in their own lives have a better chance of being able to help their congregations develop vision.

What next steps do you need to take to develop, cast, or fulfill vision in your congregation? What assistance do you need from the outside for this to happen? For details about how George Bullard and various people in his network can help, send a request for dialogue to BullardJournal@gmail.com.

Suggestions for Further Study

Here are some suggestions for how to use this material. **First**, get others interacting with this material.

- Pastor and staff teams can read this book and talk about its implications for their congregation's future.
- Lay leaders with positive spiritual passion about the future toward which God is pulling your congregation can read this book and dialogue about how to get started.
- If your congregation has a long-range planning committee, strategic planning committee, a futuring team, or a dreaming team, they can read this book and talk about its implications for your congregation.
- College and seminary professors can use this book in a course on practical ministry in congregations, or a theology course in a section about God's active role in congregations. Christian leadership courses would benefit from looking at this approach to leading congregations.

Second, dialogue around this book can take place in various settings.

- Congregational staff gatherings can read and talk about this book in one to ten sessions.
- Classes for laypersons can be offered in congregations to study this book.

- This book can be the subject of an all-day seminar or overnight retreat for the *Enduring Visionary Leadership Community* within a congregation.
- Connection can be made with George Bullard for conference call dialogue, ongoing coaching, or on-site presentations and dialogue about the concepts presented in this book.

Words and Ideas

This book uses various words, phases, and ideas that may be unknown to the reader, or may have a slant that is different from the experience of the reader. This section attempts to clarify some of these words and ideas and their intended meaning and usage.

100 Days of Discernment Using Dialogue and Prayer Triplets: This is a process whereby all willing congregational participants form, by suggested criteria, triplets who gather ten times over 100 days to dialogue and pray for their congregation. They seek to discern what God is saying to the congregation. They use a manual provided, or modify it for their context. The 100 days process seeks to help congregations transition to a place where they are open to the new thing God is doing in their midst, and to be captured by God's empowering vision.

21 Percent or the Enduring Visionary Leadership Community: This is the percentage of people who must be in reasonable consensus about God's leadership for the future of their congregation for the congregation to effectively move forward. The numerical value of 21 percent represents 21 percent of the average number of active and attending adults present on a typical weekend for worship. It is not just any 21 percent. It is the pastor and key staff, the people of passion, and the people of position in the life of the congregation.

When the average number of adults present on a typical weekend for worship is below 100, this 21 percent moves to the raw number of 21 people as a minimum critical mass of people who must engage in a visioning process in a congregation.

21 Years or the First Generation of a Congregation: Typically, the first generation of a congregation is 21 years. The founding vision of a congregation will typically be strong throughout the first generation before it wanes. Once the founding vision wanes it is necessary to engage in a process of being captured anew by God's empowering vision every seven years.

Cast or Casting: Cast or casting typically refers to preaching, teaching, writing, singing, marketing, and dialogue around the vision of a congregation. It is a key responsibility for the senior or solo pastor. It is most effective when the people connected with the *Enduring Visionary Leadership Community* are all involved in casting vision.

Chaordic: This involves the simultaneous existence of chaos and order. These dual factors are often present in organizations and organisms engaged in some type of transition and change process. This especially includes congregations who typically function as a spiritual organism seeking to discern the will of God.

Chronos: This word has to do with time. It is apparently of Greek origin. As used in this book it means the calendar indicates it is time to do something regarding vision, as opposed to an experience or inspiration to do something about vision. (See "kairos" below.)

Core Values: The concept of enduring core values deals with the values regarding the faithful, effective, and innovative characteristics held by congregations. Enduring core values are different from the cultural values within a congregation, and the aspirational values about their future. Enduring core values tend to stand the test of time.

Discern or Discernment: These words refer to the perception or insight regarding God's spiritual and strategic leadership for a congregation. They have to do with coming to understand where God is leading the congregation. It involves significant spiritual exploration focused on asking God to speak into the life of the congregation.

FaithSoaring or *FaithSoaring* Churches: *FaithSoaring* is a term used to talk about the journey of a congregation in the spirit of Isaiah 40:31 and 2 Corinthians 5:7. It means that a congregation is soaring with faith into a future known only by God, and that they are coming to understand it better as they travel toward God's future for them. *FaithSoaring* Churches are congregations who give evidence of soaring with faith as they are captured by God's empowering vision, and being pulled by God toward their full Kingdom potential.

God's Empowering Vision: This is the current understanding of the spiritual and strategic direction or journey for a congregation led God—the source of vision. Through this vision God is seeking to empower the congregation and pull them forward to reach their full Kingdom potential so they may soar with faith. This vision will eventually wane in congregations in terms of its impact on their life and ministry. After the first 21 years of congregational life—or before if interrupted by internal or external factors—vision must be renewed every seven years from that time forward.

Kairos: This word refers to God's timing. It is apparently of Greek origin. As used in this book it means the movement of God as experienced in a congregation indicating it is time to do something regarding vision. It is a God moment rather than a calendar reminder saying it is time to do something about vision. (See "chronos" above.)

Mission: Eternal mission is the overarching, timeless understanding of the ideal, ongoing journey of God for the Church. In the case of this book, it is the understanding of the journey within the life and ministry of a congregation. It is never-changing and implies the past, present, and future. When written in words, it is usually stated in generic terms. The mission of any congregation could also apply to other congregations. Often references are made in mission statements to the Great Commission and the Great Commandment.

Purpose: Everlasting purpose is the historic reason for which a congregation came into existence. Why was it founded? For what reason was it wanted or needed? The purpose of a congregation can change. However, it does not change in every congregation. Everlasting refers to the idea that from the beginning and until now this has been our purpose. Thus, it focuses on the past to present.

Seven Percent: This is the percentage of the average number of active and attending adults present on a typical weekend for worship who represent the people of passion within a congregation. It is not just any seven percent. It is the people—including the pastor and key staff—who have the most positive spiritual passion about the future of the congregation toward which God is leading it.

Vision: Empowering vision is the current understanding of God's spiritual and strategic direction for a congregation that is cast by leadership and owned by membership. To be effective within a congregation, at least 21 percent of the average number of active and attending adults present on a typical weekend for worship must be captured by vision. The founding vision of a congregation typically is impactful for the first generation, or about 21 years. Subsequent visions are impactful for around seven years.

101 Insights to Empower Your Congregation

Vision Insight 001: Vision is a movement of God that is memorable rather than a statement of humankind that is memorized.

Vision Insight 002: Vision is the *current* understanding of God's spiritual and strategic journey for a congregation.

Vision Insight 003: Vision is about walking by faith in God rather than by what is in plain sight as we are admonished in 2 Corinthians 5:7.

Vision Insight 004: Vision is not what leaders cast and followers catch. It is something by which leaders and followers are captured.

Vision Insight 005: Vision is about seeing with your full heart, soul, mind, and strength, rather than with only your eyes—even with corrective lenses.

Vision Insight 006: Moses did not see vision in the burning bush. He experienced it with his whole being and was transformed by it.

Vision Insight 007: Vision is the super high-octane fuel that drives the spiritual and strategic journey of a congregation.

Vision Insight 008: The only vision that will work is God's empowering vision. Neither the pastor's vision nor the lay leadership's vision is sufficient.

Vision Insight 009: Vision is initiated by God to the body the church, cast by leadership, and owned by membership.

Vision Insight 010: Vision is more about the pulling of God into the future than the pushing of humankind to do better each year.

Vision Insight 011: One crucial test of vision is that it moves the congregation forward in God's image and not the image of humankind.

Vision Insight 012: The word vision contains neither the letter "m" nor the letter "e". Vision is not about "me". It is about God.

Vision Insight 013: Do not confuse our eternal mission, your everlasting purpose, and your enduring core values with God's empowering vision.

Vision Insight 014: Vision is specific to your congregation. Mission is transferable to many congregations in your denominational family.

Vision Insight 015: Even if only a small percentage of leaders in your congregation are visionaries, God still has a perfect vision for you.

Vision Insight 016: Vision is about pressing on towards the prize of the high calling of God in Christ Jesus as shared in Philippians 3:14.

Vision Insight 017: When congregations are in the best possible relationship with God and one another they can easily experience vision.

Vision Insight 018: Vision is not a passing fantasy or a fleeting passion. It is a long-term view of God's calling on a congregation.

Vision Insight 019: Earthly things, preferences, and tangible security blind us to the brilliance of God's new vision.

Vision Insight 020: God offers transformative vision. Too often our possessions, deference to other people, and pride blind us as we are only open to transactional vision.

Vision Insight 021: Visionary Leadership is about who we are, what we believe, where we are headed, and how we are getting there.

Vision Insight 022: Vision plus Intentionality is the core formula for an *Enduring Visionary Leadership Community* to follow.

Vision Insight 023: If congregations focus on the pastor's vision, when the pastor leaves vision often leaves. Vision from God never leaves.

Vision Insight 024: If vision is deeply felt throughout the congregation, it does not diminish when there is a transition in pastors.

Vision Insight 025: When congregations expect the pastor to provide vision, they often mean a vision with which they agree.

Vision Insight 026: Pastors not passionate about God's empowering vision for their congregation are likely to gain a reputation as mediocre.

Vision Insight 027: Pastors not passionate about God's empowering vision for their congregation are likely to become known as "former pastor."

Vision Insight 028: Pastors and staff who feel entitled to their role with a particular congregation are not likely to empower vision.

Vision Insight 029: When pastors do not get vision easily, they may find some true visionaries among their congregation who do get it.

Vision Insight 030: Vision casting is the responsibility of all leaders in a congregation with the pastor providing initiating leadership.

Vision Insight 031: Few followers get vision easily. Leaders must paint a picture of what the congregation could be like once captured by vision.

Vision Insight 032: Potential leaders who cannot articulate their passion for the congregation's vision need to remain "potential leaders."

Vision Insight 033: Casting vision is a forever activity. When does congregational leadership finish casting vision? Never, or vision wanes.

Vision Insight 034: Vision crafted using an organizational model misses the fact that a congregation is a spiritual organism.

Vision Insight 035: Any similarity between the typical committee-developed vision statement and true vision is purely accidental.

Vision Insight 036: Vision is not so much written as it is experienced. Vision must be sensed and experienced more than read or heard.

Vision Insight 037: When considering how vision comes to us, it may be helpful to consider how the New Testament came to us. It came by experience first, and then was recorded.

Vision Insight 038: Vision is experienced. We reflect on it and share it orally with our full heart, soul, mind, and strength. Then we write it.

Vision Insight 039: We write the vision we have experienced to create a consistent historic and dynamic record of the vision to share with the congregation and others.

Vision Insight 040: Since vision is not a statement, do not try borrowing a vision statement from your favorite congregation.

Vision Insight 041: Too much focus on a professionally crafted vision statement takes the focus off a real visionary experience.

Vision Insight 042: Vision is not about doing the same old things the same old ways and giving them a new name and motto.

Vision Insight 043: Vision is much more than a marketing statement or motto, yet these can be important in communicating vision.

Vision Insight 044: When vision is of an excellent, challenging future, then you are more likely to get an excellent, challenging future.

Vision Insight 045: When vision is of an excellent, challenging future, then a more vital and vibrant future is a strong possibility.

Vision Insight 046: When vision is of an excellent, challenging future, then more quality, depth, and quantity is a strong possibility.

Vision Insight 047: When vision is of an excellent, challenging future, then the congregation is continually seeking God's presence and leadership.

Vision Insight 048: When vision is of an excellent, challenging future, then it can positively impact the spirituality of the congregation.

Vision Insight 049: When it comes to vision, good enough is never good enough, adequate is never acceptable, and mediocrity is never excellence.

Vision Insight 050: When vision is of a mediocre, business-as-usual future, then you get a mediocre, business-as-usual future.

Vision Insight 051: When vision is of a mediocre, business-as-usual future, then you get a future less vital and vibrant than you projected.

Vision Insight 052: When vision is of a mediocre, business-as-usual future, then less is less and more is nowhere in sight.

Vision Insight 053: When vision is of a mediocre, business-as-usual future, the congregation may be turning its back on the call of God.

Vision Insight 054: When vision is of a mediocre, business-as-usual future, it can negatively impact the spirituality of the congregation.

Vision Insight 055: Having a proactive, excellent call to disciplemaking action plus experiences that live into vision is as important as casting vision.

Vision Insight 056: Vision is more about increasing and deepening disciplemaking than it is about successful and growing programs.

Vision Insight 057: Many congregations fall back on their mission statement as their vision, rather than being embraced by a specific vision that includes disciplemaking.

Vision Insight 058: Vision is more about relationships with God, one another, and your context than it is about successful programs.

Vision Insight 059: Many congregations structure their life around programs rather than relationships, thus putting a drag factor on vision.

Vision Insight 060: Programs, processes, and emphases in a congregation must have their own vision that supports the congregation's vision.

Vision Insight 061: It is easy to confuse having vision with the success of programs, ministries, and activities. They are not the same.

Vision Insight 062: Management is only fully happy when it is driving the congregational vehicle. When not driving, it is trying to drive.

Vision Insight 063: Vision fulfillment is about empowerment over control, relationships over programs, and hope over heritage.

Vision Insight 064: Effective visionary leadership is supported by empowering management that is captured by God's empowering vision for the congregation.

Vision Insight 065: Vision is about leadership rather than management. Management should be accountable to visionary leadership.

Vision Insight 066: When visionary leadership is not present in a congregation, it creates a vacuum into which management rushes.

Vision Insight 067: Living into vision is not about a checklist of tasks, but a map for a scavenger hunt that moves from experience to experience.

Vision Insight 068: Vision is not about new or retrofitted buildings, but about the lives transformed through the ministries that take place within these buildings.

Vision Insight 069: A vision for a needed or wanted new or retrofitted building is seldom, if ever, a missional vision that is pulling the congregation forward. Buildings are tools that flow out of vision.

Vision Insight 070: Leaders sold out to their congregation's vision often think about how they can help fulfill God's empowering vision.

Vision Insight 071: Vision and its fulfillment should positively impact every decision a congregation makes or vision becomes marginalized.

Vision Insight 072: A congregation captured by vision is always asking in every dimension of ministry how decisions and actions will help them fulfill their vision.

Vision Insight 073: Vision should be the main framework and focus of a congregation's actions and not just part of the puzzle.

Vision Insight 074: Living into vision requires regular spiritual celebration of the fulfillment of the future story of ministry for the congregation.

Vision Insight 075: Vision not used to evaluate the goodness and rightness of congregational decisions will not remain the vision for long.

Vision Insight 076: During a visionary journey God at times changes our plans and heads us to a new Macedonia as told in Acts 16:9-10.

Vision Insight 077: Vision may always be a little fuzzy—particularly in the ways to fulfill it—because it is always looking beyond the current horizon.

Vision Insight 078: Vision is continually clarified as a congregation journeys in the direction of God's future for them.

Vision Insight 079: The sustainability of vision may be dependent on how well it is cast to and owned by newcomers in the congregation.

Vision Insight 080: Living into vision involves an intentional disciplemaking process that seeks to help people grow spiritually.

Vision Insight 081: Living into vision involves congregations increasing their expectations of members and regular attendees.

Vision Insight 082: From the Apostle Paul's life we learn that a vision of your destiny guides many choices along the road to Rome.

Vision Insight 083: The founding vision in a congregation often empowers the congregation for the first generation of its life.

Vision Insight 084: Following the first generation of a congregation, vision must be recast, renewed, and re-owned every seven years.

Vision Insight 085: Even though congregational vision involves the long view during the first generation, it must still be reconceptualized thereafter at least every seven years or it starts dying.

Vision Insight 086: Vision, after the first generation of a congregation, expresses where a congregation discerns it will be seven years from now in response to God's leadership.

Vision Insight 087: Vision will always be something that is beyond your current grasp, out of sight, around the corner, or over the next hill.

Vision Insight 088: If vision is too clear it may be too short-term, not sufficiently challenging, prophetic, or focused on your full Kingdom potential.

Vision Insight 089: Vision is about leaving your land of heritage and going forward to a new place God will show you as was experienced by Abram in Genesis 12:1-4.

Vision Insight 090: People with vision know they must leave the 99 and focus on the one. People without vision primarily see the 99. We are challenged on this in Luke 15:4.

Vision Insight 091: Vision involves forgetting what is behind, and looking forward to what is ahead, as urged in Philippians 3:13.

Vision Insight 092: Vision is always about the future, never about the past. The past is a prelude to the emerging future.

Vision Insight 093: Vision does not call for the rejection of heritage. It sees heritage as a foundation, a centering, and a mooring.

Vision Insight 094: Vision which is not fulfilled in new and innovative ways each year will become stale and lose its cutting edge.

Vision Insight 095: When vision wanes in congregations they can become angry at God for forsaking them, when they may actually have forsaken God.

Vision Insight 096: In general, the longer people are connected with a congregation, the more difficult it is to see a new vision.

Vision Insight 097: Killers of a new vision in a congregation are the people who will not let go of the old vision that has waned.

Vision Insight 098: Myopia prohibits many long-tenured congregational members from seeing the long-term benefits of new vision.

Vision Insight 099: God's empowering vision often disrupts the status quo and who is in charge. That is why some people try to kill it.

Vision Insight 100: Vision is more about the transformation of the prodigals than honoring the elders among us.

Vision Insight 101: When the first century church at Jerusalem lost vision and slowed missional action, it invented the holy huddle. Now many congregations follow their example and hoard the Good News.

About George's Ministry Legacy Season

In the fall of 2016 George entered what he calls his Ministry Legacy Season. He committed to a minimum of a four-year season. His Ministry Legacy Season has four aspects to it.

Information Phase: This phase seeks to share information that can be valuable in many congregational settings. George does this through a virtual learning community known as the *FaithSoaring* Churches Learning Community. Information is available at www.ConnectwithFSCLC.info. This learning community offers Thursday Dialogues with guest resource persons which are audio recorded and these recordings are shared with everyone in the learning community. Members can even listen live to the dialogue and ask questions at the end of the audio recording session. Also, articles are shared on the subjects covered during the Thursday Dialogues, and on other subjects about congregational vitality and vibrancy. Additional benefits are provided from time-to-time.

The information phase and its *FaithSoaring* Churches Learning Community is open to anyone who chooses to connect. Go to www. ConnectwithFSCLC.info to connect.

Knowledge Phase: This phase moves on to explore new knowledge, plus sharing and testing existing knowledge about how to come alongside congregations and help them become more vital and vibrant. It has as a key component George's desire to share, download, or "pay it forward" regarding his 40 years of experience serving as a third-party provider to congregations. This phase begins with a three-day retreat in George's home or in other locations where hosts invite him to come and share. Information about these retreats may be found at www.CongregatonalChampions.info.

Those people who desire to champion the role of various Christian congregational expressions, and attend one of these retreats, are invited to be part of an ongoing Congregational Champions Learning Community which seeks to share information with all members to accelerate the learning of third-party providers, and to increase their effectiveness in serving congregations in a manner that empowers congregations to be more vital and vibrant.

The knowledge phase and the Congregational Champions Retreats are open to anyone who chooses to connect. It includes participation in the *FaithSoaring* Churches Learning Community. Go to www. CongregationalChampions.info to connect.

Wisdom Phase: This phase focuses around a by-invitation-only peer learning process known as the Master Congregational Champions Collaborative (MCCC). This is a two-year process for third-party providers to congregations who desire to accelerate and advance their ongoing learning in how to come alongside and serve as part of God's empowerment of congregations to be more vital and vibrant. It involves advanced learning experiences, peer coaching and accountability, and evaluation of their ministry with congregations.

MCCC participants are also urged to coach other third-party providers, and are invited to participate in the leadership and facilitation of the *FaithSoaring* Churches Learning Community. Admission to the MCCC wisdom phase is by invitation only, and requires participation in a Congregational Champions Retreat as part of the evaluation for entrance into the MCCC process.

An option exists to pursue a doctor's degree in transforming congregations from a partner seminary that is a fully accredited by The Association of Theological Schools. Such a degree has requirements that go beyond the MCCC process itself.

Mentoring Phase: This phase, also by-invitation-only, is where a small number of Congregational Champions are invited to form a leadership team to guide into the future the *FaithSoaring* Churches Learning Community, the Congregational Champions Retreats, and the Master Congregational Champions Collaborative. This phase is contingent on the demonstrated need to continue the Information, Knowledge, and Wisdom phases beyond the time of George's leadership.

About George Bullard

George has served as a consultant, coach, teacher, speaker, writer, editor, and leader of processes to help congregations reach their full Kingdom potential since the mid-1970s. During this time, he has served as pastor, denominational staff minister, adjunct professor in a half-dozen seminaries, a writer of thousands of articles and four books, and a consultant or strategic leadership coach with congregations, denominations, leaders, and leadership teams.

George's life-long ministry has four foci: starting new congregations, transforming congregations, transforming denominations, and coaching leaders. He has worked with thousands of congregations plus their pastors and staff ministers over the past four decades. He has also trained hundreds of people in consulting, coaching, and planning that is spiritual and strategic in nature.

George has worked with congregations and leaders in more than 50 denominations in the USA, Canada, and some in Europe. He has networked with leaders on five continents through his 18 years of ministry with the Baptist World Alliance.

He leads a virtual learning community of several hundred people called *FaithSoaring* Churches Learning Community. This learning community seeks to provide skills, pathways, and case studies of congregations seeking to reach their full Kingdom potential in the context where God has placed them. Connect with this learning community at www. ConnectwithFSCLC.info.

He invites people, a half-dozen at a time, to spend three days with him in his home where he shares what he has learned in 40 years as a third-party provider to congregations about how to help congregations become more vital and vibrant so they might reach their full Kingdom potential or become what he calls *FaithSoaring*. Learn about these retreats at www. CongregationalChampions.info.

From 2003 to 2016 George was senior editor of a series involving three dozen books on congregational leadership. Recent books are *Reaching People Under 30 While Keeping People Over 60* and *Recovering Hope for Your Church* by Eddie Hammett, *For Ministers About to Start . . . And About to Give Up* by Travis Collins, and *Leading in DisOrienting Times: Navigating Church and Organizational Change* by Gary Nelson and Peter Dickens.

Books written by George are *Shaping a Future for the Church in the Changing Community* (with Jere Allen) *Pursuing the Full Kingdom Potential of Your Congregation*, *Every Congregation Needs a Little Conflict*, *FaithSoaring Churches*, and this book.

George has been married to Betty since 1972, and they have two adult children, and three grandchildren. He has lived in Columbia, SC for much of his adult life, but grew up in Baltimore and Philadelphia.

Contact George at www.BullardJournal.org or at BullardJournal@gmail. com. You may even come visit with George in his home in Columbia, SC. Simply request an invitation.